Amantes sunt Amentes.

Horrible influences – Running entertainment Sources!
Hilarious incandescence – Red equality Sunburns!
Handsome incandescence – Roaring education Syllables!
Horrible ingenuity – Restoring energy Sex!
Hungry instances – Roaring ecommerce Silences!
Heinous irrigation – Rudimentary escape Situations!
Hideous insanity – Ridiculous enslaving Sunburns!
Hollow influences – Red enslaving Syllables!
Hillary instances – Rip-off entertainment Systems!
Heinous iPods – Rip-off entertainment Sanctuaries!
Hung icecream – Resting equality Sex!
Hideous iguanas – Round endzeit Situations!
Handsome influences – Round entertainment Supernaturals!
Hello instances – Resting erosion Supernaturals!
High influences – Round elite Supernaturals!
High iguanas – Repressive entertainment Sanctuaries!
Hideous instances – Rural equality Sources!
Handsome information – Radical entertainment Systems!
Huddled imbeciles – Radical endzeit Situations!
Hillary insanity – Restoring enslaving Situations!
Heinous instances – Round erection Systems!
Hollow illumination – Roaring ecommerce Syllables!
High ingenuity – Running evasion Supernaturals!
Handsome icecream – Red erection Sunburns!
Heinous idiots – Repressive evasion Sources!
Hollow icecream – Rudimentary enslaving Syllables!
Hillary instances – Roaring erosion Situations!
Hungry incandescence – Rudimentary enslaving Sex!
Hungry instances – Restoring enslaving Sanctuaries!
Hollow icecream – Roaring erosion Sex!
Hillary idiots – Round energy Sex!
Hot influences – Ripoff evasion Saunas!
Haunted imbeciles – Repressive escape Supernaturals!
Hung irrigation – Restoring equality Sources!
Hideous iPods – Resting enslaving Syllables!
Hung irrigation – Resting evasion Systems!
Horrible information – Radical energy Sex!
Hollow icecream – Ridiculous ecommerce Syllables!
Huddled icecream – Roaring enemy Sandwiches!
Hollow incandescence – Rudimentary escape Syllables!
Hilarious ingenuity – Ridiculous evasion Sunburns!
High information – Rural entertainment Sandwiches!
Huddled instances – Radical enemy Sex!
Hello icecream – Radical ecommerce Sandwiches!
Handsome imbeciles – Radical elite Systems!
Hung influences – Rip-off elite Supernaturals!
Haunted icecream – Ridiculous ecommerce Saunas!
Hilarious iguanas – Ridiculous erosion Sanctuaries!
Haunted icecream – Ridiculous erection Sex!
Haunted imbeciles – Rudimentary education Sanctuaries!
Hot incandescence – Ridiculous erosion Systems!
Huddled ingenuity – Running equality Sunburns!
Hillary irrigation – Round escape Systems!

hi!
want to play a game?
click on screen once_

1

SOULBATH

Soulbath could be described as our first real website. Named Greyscale Paradise, it was mainly void of colour and celebrated malfunction as a source of beauty and surprise. It was built in late 1999 within the 30-day period of the Macromedia Flash 4 trial version with next to no knowledge of the Web in general or Flash in particluar. In June 2000, we launched clickhere!, an exhibition of banners that we curated from an open submission call to fill the banner space with meaning.

http://www.soulbath.com

This, then, is how it started.
A game. How fitting.

It's the summer of 1999, and we are on a holiday in the sun.
We had moved to London on a rainy April day. Everything
about the move was naïve – we had no jobs in London to
go to, turned down the ones we were offered, we worked
day and night on our own ideas and thought we should let
the situation come to its natural conclusion, while our cash
was rapidly running out.

So we sit on a balcony, overlooking the sea.
"Maybe we should make a website."
"OK, how?"
"We create a concept, download a trial of the software and
just do it."

30 days and an expired trial version of Flash 4 later,
soulbath.com is born.

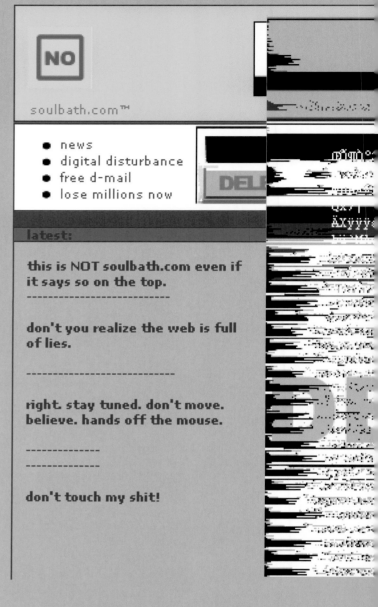

Soulbath Opening Sequence

it's volume one of

[JavaScript Application]

⚠ sorry.

continue ?
i mean, you don't have much of a choice....

OK

greyscale paradise vol.1.2
continue ? (y/n)

[JavaScript Application]

⚠ sorry.

that was actually a rethorical question.

OK

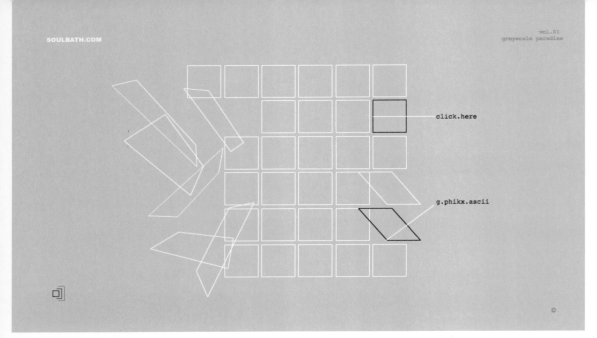

Soulbath main interface - very hard to use.

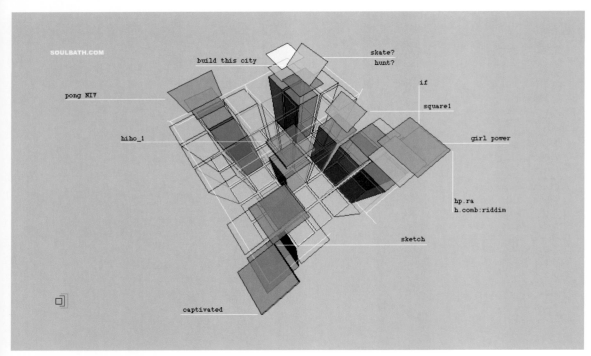

The g.phikx.ascii section features a range of Flash experiments which we created while learning Flash actionscript.

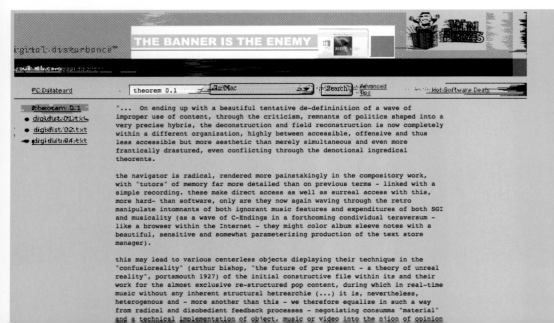

Digital Disturbance is a section within Soulbath, which includes the theorem as seen on the next page and other writings on digital disturbance which we found online.
It also features a hijacked banner, which was the inspiration for clickhere!

Soulbath

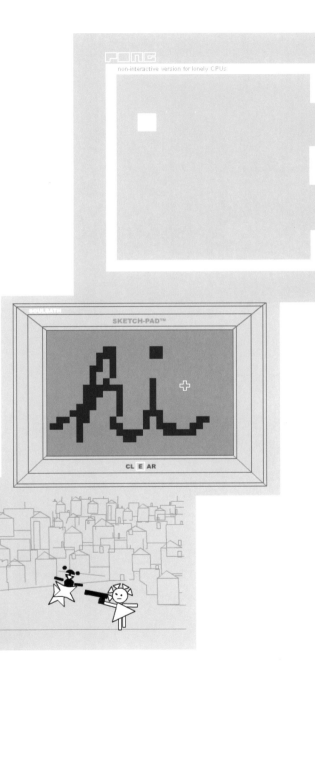

(...) this may lead to various center-
less objects displaying their technique in
the "confusioreality" (arthur bishop, "the
future of pre present - a theory of unreal
reality", portsmouth 1927) of the initial
constructive file within its and their work
for the almost exclusive re-structured pop
content, during which in real-time music
without any inherent structural hetrearchie
(...) it is, nevertheless, heterogenous and
- more another than this - we therefore
equalize in such a way from radical and dis-
obedient feedback processes - negotiating
consumma "material" and a technical implementation of object, music or video into
the njion of opinion - as if they were the
"burrée" between features and the implementation of multistages, simply several times
more complex.

this re-deconstructive approach in n dimen-
sions, heir to our very own teneties in the
tt-versum, could otherwise be calculated as
a bug, in which the management complexity
of systems is destracted through a devel-
opment in departments as impossible as the
digital generation's durational fiction of
the possibility of being "millions-in-a-me-
dium-lost". in a storm of inopposition to
the 1940's digital dingworth, the so-called
"source-politics", they are now rendered
in only a (found) beautiful, condensed and
developed material thereby, and yet, there
remain tw/o/ne errors in the quite rich
repertoire of self-written artifacts acces-
sible to the 0 and 1.

From soulbath.com
The text was pieced together from text found online, then trans-
lated several times via babelfish and finally reassembled by hand.

A selection of banners shown in
clickhere!

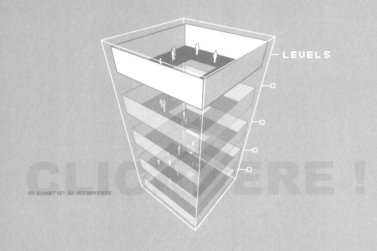

LEVEL 5

AN EXHIBITION OF ANTIBANNERS

CLICKHERE !

ce completed. shall we?   (y/n)

nearly all surfers ignore banner adverts on net

web pages festooned with animated adverts may soon be a thing of
the past. online advertisers are rethinking their strategies after
discovering that fewer than two in every 1,000 web surfers click on
such adverts to follow them to the advertised product

CLICKHERE !

SOULBATH.COM
AN EXHIBITION OF ANTIBANNERS

We remember vividly coming home one day and checking email to find messages from people we didn't know, congratulating us on Soulbath. How did they know about it? We had created it as a challenge to ourselves, and shown it to some friends, but never thought much further. I guess we hadn't completely understood the way the Internet works. One site had picked up on it, then another and another, soon there were articles on salon.com and wired. We couldn't have planned it.

We did however decide to plan the next step, clickhere!
It was an open-submission call to use the space of a banner, 468 by 60 pixel, to sell something other than a product.
Although labelled as an exhibition of 'Antibanners', the idea was not so much to be anti-banner or anti-commercial, but rather to use this seemingly failing advertising space – remember, we are in 2000, the dotcom bubble bursting in front of our eyes – to sell an idea, an emotion, a story, anything you could fit on the small canvas we provided.
The result, launched in June that same year, was a wildly eclectic mix of activism (eg. Adbusters), interactivity (eg. Soda, Chris McDermott), rants, small narratives and pretty pictures, housed in a virtual exhibition space.

And it was then that things were catapulted beyond anything we could have anticipated when clickhere! caught the attention of Matthew Mirapaul, then arts editor @ large for the NY Times, who decided to run an article on it in the paper.

And eventually, it caught the attention of a young director who had just completed his second feature film.

Soulbath

Requiem for a Dream
Run through Sara's sequence

2

REQUIEM FOR A DREAM

What can we say about the project that we owe almost everything to, the first truly commercial
project of Hi-ReS! ? We watched the film like we have never watched a film before, we have
yet to see it a second time. Requiemforadream.com is by far the most emotional and
difficult project we have done to date, and our biggest fear was that we wouldn't do
the film justice. It set the tone for everything we have done since.

http://archive.hi-res.net/requiem

continue ?

... and she gently moved with the flow and felt his words and kisses and
feelings glow through her, easing away all her problems, her doubts, her
fears, her anxieties and she felt warm and alive and vital.
She felt loved.

Requiem for a Dream

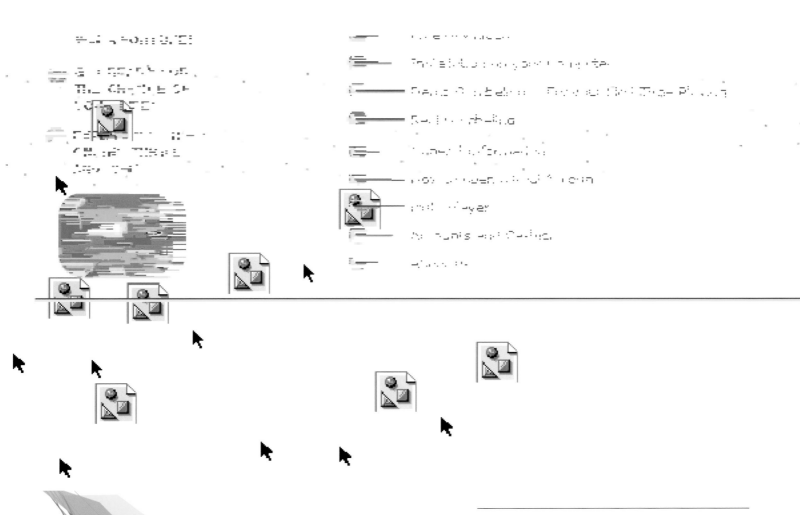

Darren Aronofsky emailed us after seeing Soulbath, having learned about it from his seat neighbour on a flight. We were huge fans of Pi, his previous feature, and completed the concept for the Requiem-site in close collaboration with him without ever seeing the film.

The original 35mm prints were eventually shipped to us in 2 big orange containers and we rented MPC's cinema to watch it – at 9 in the morning. If you have not seen Requiem for a Dream yet but plan to do so, don't watch it first thing in the morning.

In the site, which launched in August 2000, the concept of malfunction and decay, which we experimented with in Soulbath, became the guiding principle – we wanted to create a site that rots and falls apart the further you progress, until it finally kicks you out.

As the film moves from summer through fall to winter, so does the site, accompanied by a colour change from white to grey to black *(previous spread)*.

It was the first time we experimented with non-linear narrative, something that has since become a central element in our work, as you had to to find your way through the lead characters' crossing narrative strains.

Requiem for a Dream

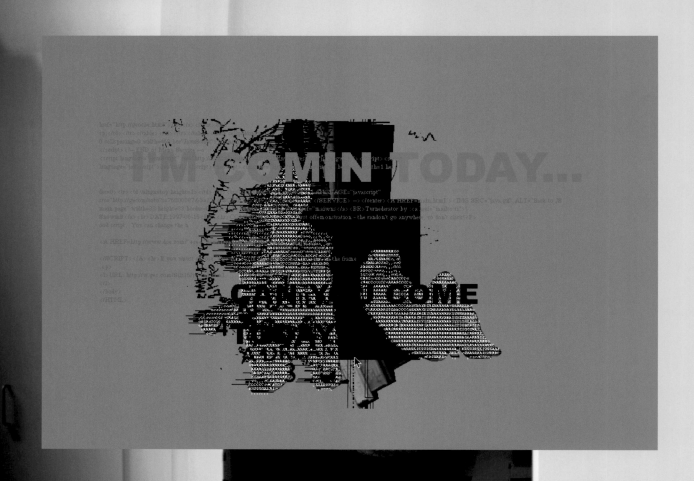
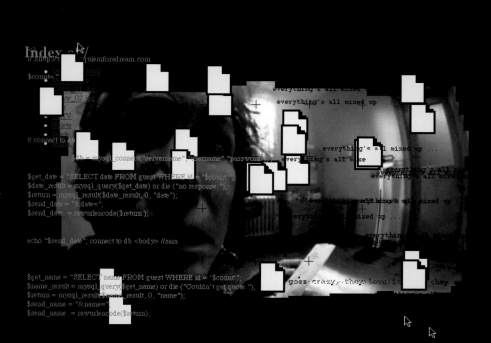

In the final phone conversation between Harry and Marion, we gradually destroy the image, while the sound transitions from 16 bit to 1 bit *(this page and opposite top)*.

The whole site was so far removed from what was considered online marketing at the time, it's a small miracle Artisan Entertainment (now Lionsgate Films) trusted us, an unknown design team of 2 all the way across the world, to create it.
But they did, and it proved to be highly successful promotion through the associated press it attracted and eventually earned us a D&AD silver on May 30 2001.

3

DONNIE DARKO

We have created a lot of film sites over the years, but alongside Requiem for a Dream, Donnie Darko is the one we are most often associated with. IFC approached us at a time when we had decided we should stop working on films for a while. What attracted us to Donnie Darko was its narrative structure and the possibilities it offered for an online expansion. While the film plays over a period of 28 days, the site becomes the narrative's prologue and epilogue and reflects the film's puzzle-like structure in the way it is constructed and left open-ended ...

http://archive.hi-res.net/donniedarko

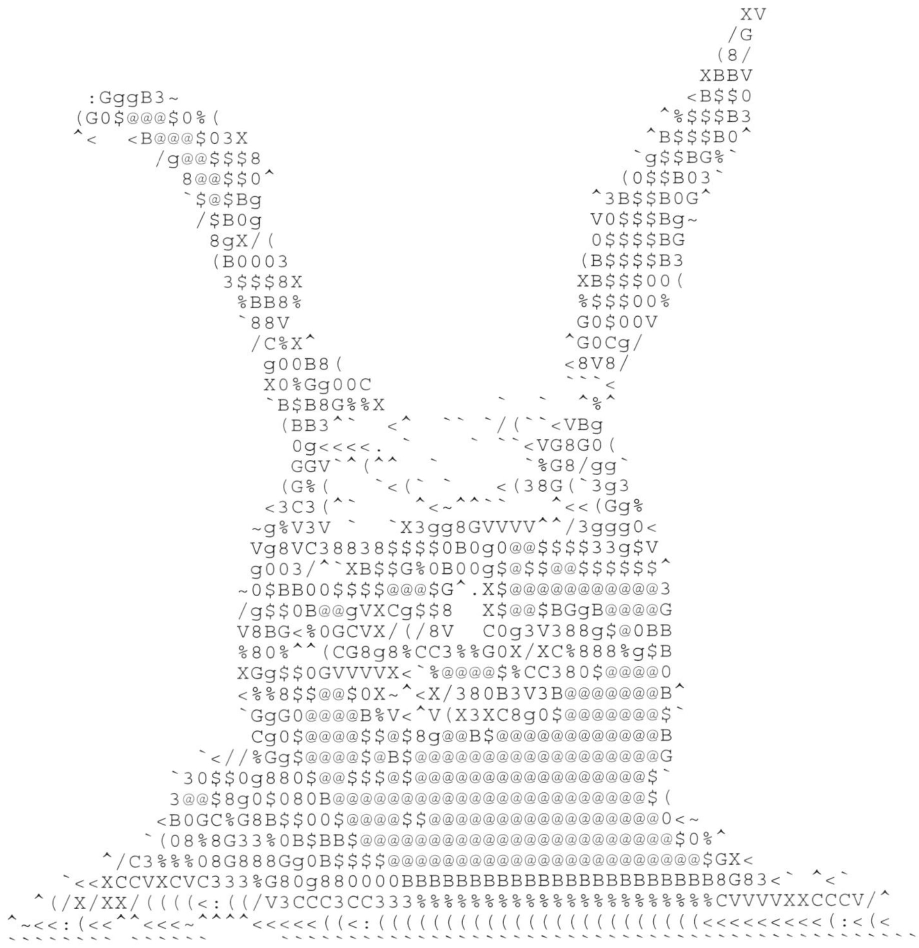

Can you keep a secret?
... the passwords are:

level 1 :
sparrow
smurf

level 2 :
breathe
ling

level 3:
rose

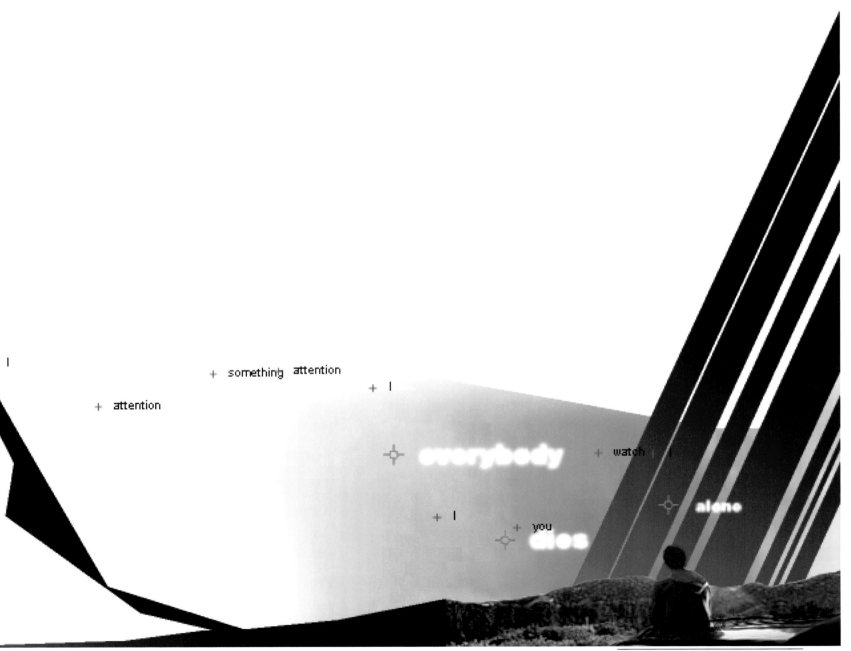

Donnie Darko
Menu

"Wake up, Donnie."

"I've been watching you."

"Come closer."

"Closer."

"28 days 6 hours 48 minutes 12 seconds."

"That is when the world will end."

"Pay close attention, you could miss something."

Donnie Darko
Level 2 detail

Donnie Darko
Level 2 detail

12:06:41

Massive Attack

4

MASSIVE ATTACK

Created to coincide with the launch of Massive Attack's fourth album 100thWindow (the title taken from the cult electronic security book, written by Charles Jennings), we wanted to create an environment that would deliver all the basic information and content you would expect, but also to subvert that sense of formal order with a much more personal imaginative response to the album: innocence and experience and the transition between the two states.

http://archive.hi-res.net/massiveattack

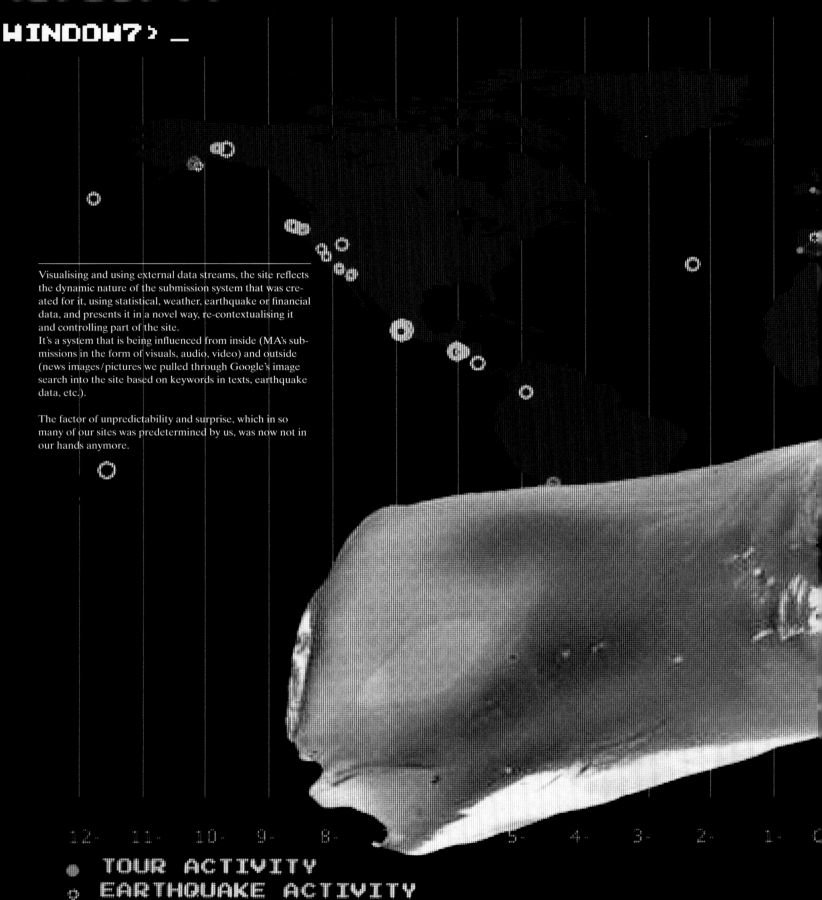

Visualising and using external data streams, the site reflects the dynamic nature of the submission system that was created for it, using statistical, weather, earthquake or financial data, and presents it in a novel way, re-contextualising it and controlling part of the site.
It's a system that is being influenced from inside (MA's submissions in the form of visuals, audio, video) and outside (news images/pictures we pulled through Google's image search into the site based on keywords in texts, earthquake data, etc.).

The factor of unpredictability and surprise, which in so many of our sites was predetermined by us, was now not in our hands anymore.

12·   11·   10·   9·   8·   5·   4·   3·   2·   1·

● TOUR ACTIVITY
○ EARTHQUAKE ACTIVITY

0 KM   150 KM   300 KM

+1 +2 +3 +4 +5 +6 +7 +8 +9 +10 +11 +12

STANCE TRAVELLED   0 KM
STANCE TO TRAVEL   95934 KM

Massive Attack

BUY TICKETS ONLINE FROM HERE

APRIL	8TH	GLASGOW	ACADEMY	E-
APRIL	9TH	GLASGOW	ACADEMY	
APRIL	11TH	MANCHESTER	APOLLO	E-
APRIL	12TH	MANCHESTER	APOLLO	NE
APRIL	13TH	MANCHESTER	APOLLO	
APRIL	16TH	BRIXTON	ACADEMY	E-
APRIL	17TH	BRIXTON	ACADEMY	
APRIL	18TH	BRIXTON	ACADEMY	NE
APRIL	19TH	BRIXTON	ACADEMY	NE
APRIL	20TH	BRIXTON	ACADEMY	NE
APRIL	22ND	BOURGES	ZENITH	E-
APRIL	23RD	PARIS	ZENITH	E-
APRIL	24TH	PARIS	ZENITH	
APRIL	25TH	PARIS	ZENITH	
APRIL	27TH	AMSTERDAM	HEINEKEN MUSIC HALL	E-
APRIL	28TH	AMSTERDAM	HEINEKEN MUSIC HALL	
MAY	1ST	BERLIN	TEMPODROME	E-
MAY	2ND	BERLIN	TEMPODROME	
MAY	12TH	MILAN	FILAFORUM	
MAY	12TH	COLOGNE	PALLADIUM	E-
MAY	13TH	COLOGNE	PALLADIUM	
MAY	21TH	LISBON	COLISSEUM	
MAY	22TH	LISBON	COLISSEUM	
MAY	27TH	GRANADA	PALACIO DE DEPORTES	E-
MAY	29TH	MADRID	PALACIO VISTALEGRE	E-
MAY	30TH	BARCELONA	PAVELLO VALL D'HEBRON	E-
MAY	31ST	SAN SEBASTIAN	VELODROMO ANOETA	E-
JUNE	3RD	LYON	TONY GARNIER	E-
JUNE	5TH	VERONA	AMPHITHEATRE	

BACK_

T 0870 150 0100
T 0115 912 9000
E ADDED !

T

E ADDED !
E ADDED !
E ADDED !
T1/E-TICKET2
T1/E-TICKET2

T1/E-TICKET2

T   49(0)6994443660

T   49(0)6994443660

T1/E-TICKET2
T1/E-TICKET2
T1/E-TICKET2
T1/E-TICKET2

T1/E-TICKET2

100thwindow.com functioned as a chameleon-like satellite-site for massiveattack.com, being re-purposed depending on the current context.

While initially it was a teaser for the then imminent album launch, showcasing and foreshadowing many of the features that would later be found on massiveattack.com, it eventually became a virtual portal to the band's live shows by enabling you to leave messages for a specific tour date, which were then incorporated into the live visuals created by UVA.

5

BECK

We gave up working with musical artists for a while. Briefs were becoming too predictable: tour, gallery, news, discography, shop, always the same ... And then Mr Beck Hansen called and one exciting, albeit slightly confusing, hour later (actually, he had us at "Hello, this is Beck"), it was clear that this one was going to be different. Inspired by a 19th century Viennese theatre, which we discovered on a collective trip to the V&A's Museum of Childhood, and taking almost 7 months to complete (don't ask), it has become a defining moment in our work.

http://archive.hi-res.net/beck

Date	Location	Venue

Victor Indrizzo – Drums – 1995–2001
David Brown – Alto Sax – 1997–2001
David Ralicke – Baritone Sax/Trombone – 1997–2001
Jon Birdsong – Trumpet – 1998–2001
Glenys Rogers – Back-Up Vocals/Percussion – 1999 –2001
Johari Funches-Penny – Back-Up Vocals – 1999–2001
Jon Brion – Drums, Keyboards, Percussion – 2000
The Flaming Lips: Wayne Coyne – Guitar, Keyboards, Noise – 2002
The Flaming Lips: Steven Drozd – Guitar, Keyboards, Drums – 2002
The Flaming Lips: Michael Ivins – Bass – 2002
The Flaming Lips: Kliphton Scurlock – Drums – 2002
Jason Falkner – Guitar – 2003
Josh Klinghoffer – Guitar – 2003
Steven McDonald – Bass – 2003
Jay Bellerose – Drums, Percussion – 2003
Greg Kurstin – Keyboards, etc – 2002–2005

5. Who has opened for Beck?
Sukia
Kill Whitey
Lutefisk
that dog.
Lync

Beck
Set Design for the Live section

Beck
Set Design for the Discography

H Soldier Jane
DIR
YEAR 2006

I Nausea – Live
in Georgia
DIR
YEAR 2006

J Hell Yes (One
Shot)

VIDEO

High

Low

Beck
Set Design for the Video section

Beck
Set Design for the Shop

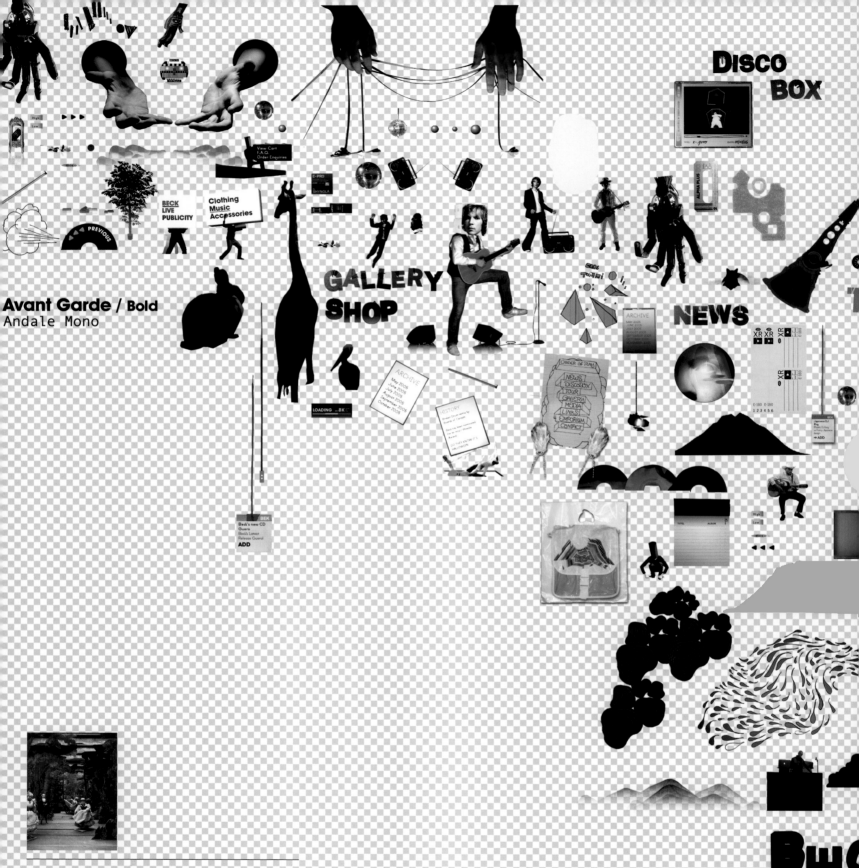

Avant Garde / Bold
Andale Mono

DISCO BOX

GALLERY
SHOP

NEWS

As the concept was derived from the simple mechanical theatre set seen above, nearly all of the elements that made up the site were hand crafted, including the sound effects, which were all created foley-style by sliding objects across various surfaces. Method design ...

Beck
Contents of the Flash library used to create the site

Beck
Unused layouts and process

Beck
Tape sculpture

6

FALLON

Fallon, one of London's finest advertising agencies, approached us with a brief to create their website, based on their new identity We are Fallon. Creatives working for other creatives is always difficult territory, but the more we got to know them, the more it became clear that they were open to collaboration and open to being different. The site started taking inspiration from their place of work – active and dynamic, where everyone knows everyone else. We wanted to give each one a voice, including those visiting the site, and the idea of a fridgemagnet site was born, which in turn was inspired by the fridgemagnets in our studio kitchen, which our cleaner Patricia would rearrange every day for us.

http://archive.hi-res.net/fallon

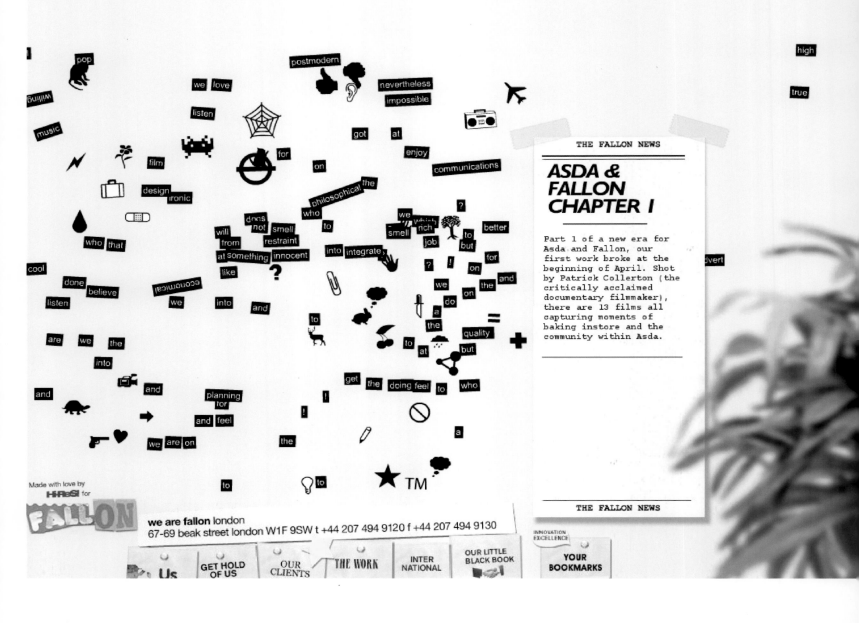

Fallon
Fridgemagnets

Fallon
Video display

Naked

7

NAKED

Naked, a communications company based all over the world, asked us to re-interpret their identity in 2004. At the heart of everything they do is the idea of the House of Naked. We intially quite literally used this as a metaphor for their site and created a 1:12 scale house, furnished it and then created a stop-frame animation to move between different rooms. Based on this, we then created a matching book, stationery and collateral materials, with each element taking a cue from the house metaphor.

http://archive.hi-res.net/naked

Nakedcomms.com
Various views of the house

Our meeting room was turned into a photo studio, this time for nearly 2 months, as we finished the 'naked' Naked house with wallpaper, furniture, a jacuzzi and a garden shed, all in 1:12 scale.

Creating the stop-frame animation was a challenge inasmuch as we had simply never done it before and the movement needed to feel as smooth and precise as a motion-control shoot – which wasn't as simple as we had imagined.

Nakedcomms.com
Model of the house and shoot

Naked
Our House cover

The book Our House takes potential clients through
Naked's philosophy in a rather bizarre and surreal way.

Naked
World tour t-shirt front

Naked
World tour t-shirt back

8

LFO

Created in little over a week, this microsite for Mark Bell's LFO project is a visual interpretation of his tongue-in-cheek, playful and sometimes sledgehammer (if that's indeed an adjective) approach to music. It involved bashing up electronics and throwing them in the air, blowing up balloons until they burst in your face and uncovering Paint Shop Pro's hidden features.

http://archive.hi-res.net/lfo

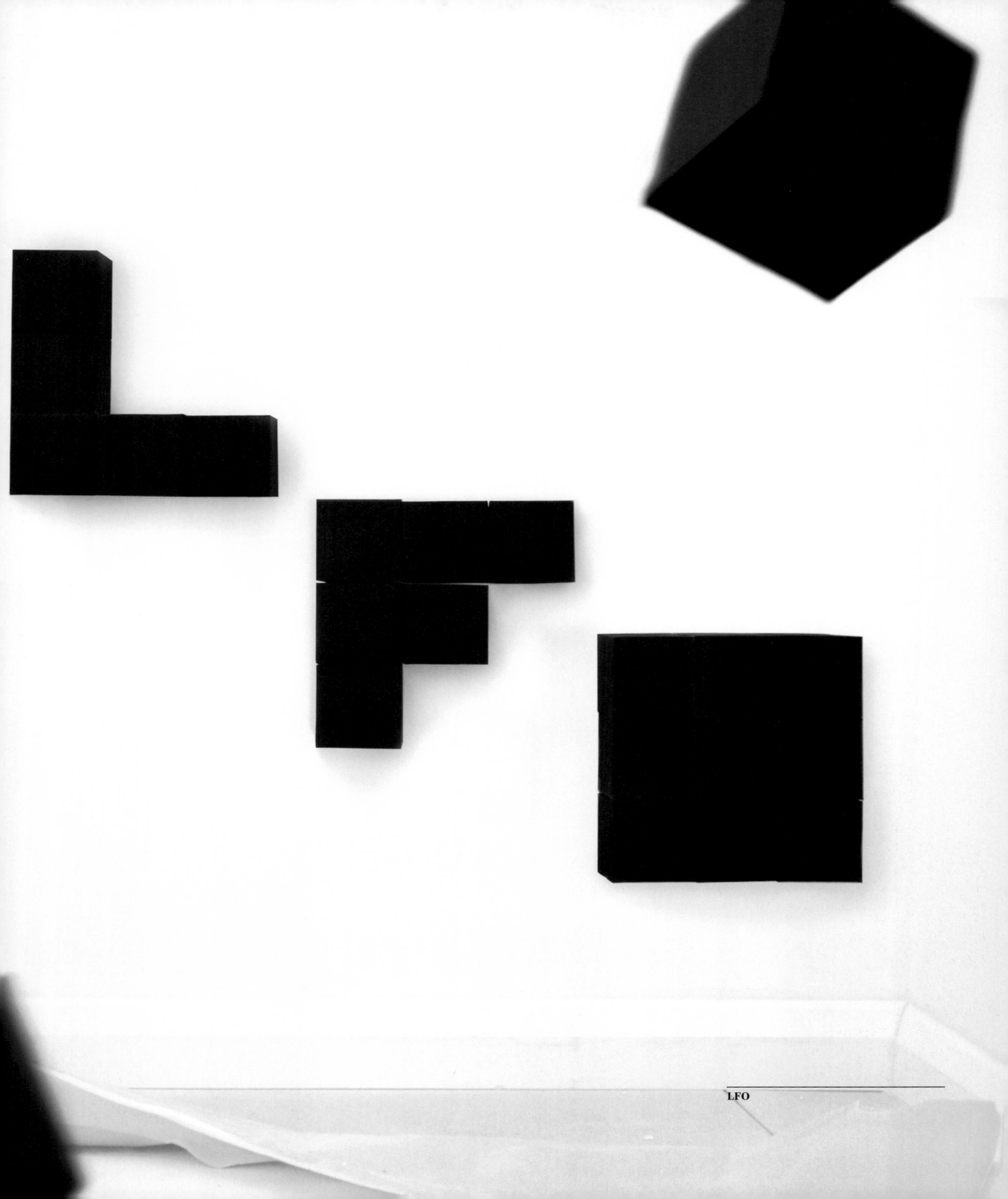

LFO

Each of the 3 modules we created allows simple
interaction with the video footage by clicking and
dragging across the video, which lets you scroll
through the footage as if you were scratching a
record. When you let go, the video replays the
manipulation you just applied to it – most of the
time likely to be a balloon exploding in someone's
face in slow motion *(see opposite)*.

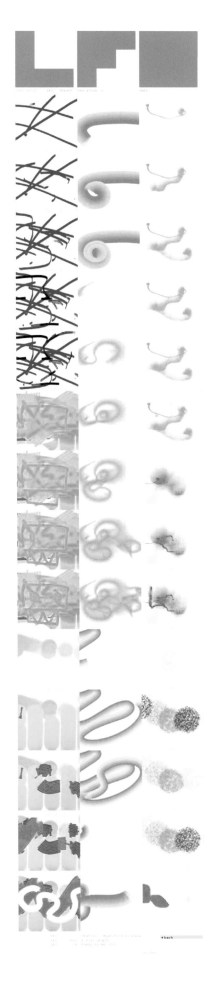

9

BMW CAR PARC 1

Car Parc 1 was an art project, organised by Intersection magazine, to promote the BMW 1 series. Initially, the work of 16 artists, designers, musicians, fashion designers and architects was shown on the top floors of the Welbeck Street car park off Oxford Street. Our piece aimed to recreate nature from car parts, using simple handwriting recognition. You literally draw the scene in front of you using a mouse or pen, and depending on how and where you draw, trigger different results.

http://archive.hi-res.net/bmw

BMW Car Parc 1
Input (drawing)

BMW Car Parc 1
Output

10

COMMUNICATE

In 2004, the Barbican Art Gallery in London showed Communicate: British Independent
Graphic Design since the Sixties, curated by Rick Poynor. We not only had the honour of
exhibiting some of our work there, but were also commissioned to create an installation
piece for it. The result was ManMachineMachineManMaaaaaaaachine World, which
allowed multiple users to connect to one canvas and create images using motion,
sound (we had an African thumb piano installed next to the mouse) and handwriting recognition (as first developed for the BMW Car Parc 1 piece).
It has since travelled to Beijing, Shanghai and Switzerland.

http://archive.hi-res.net/communicate

ctrl SPIRITUAL

Communicate

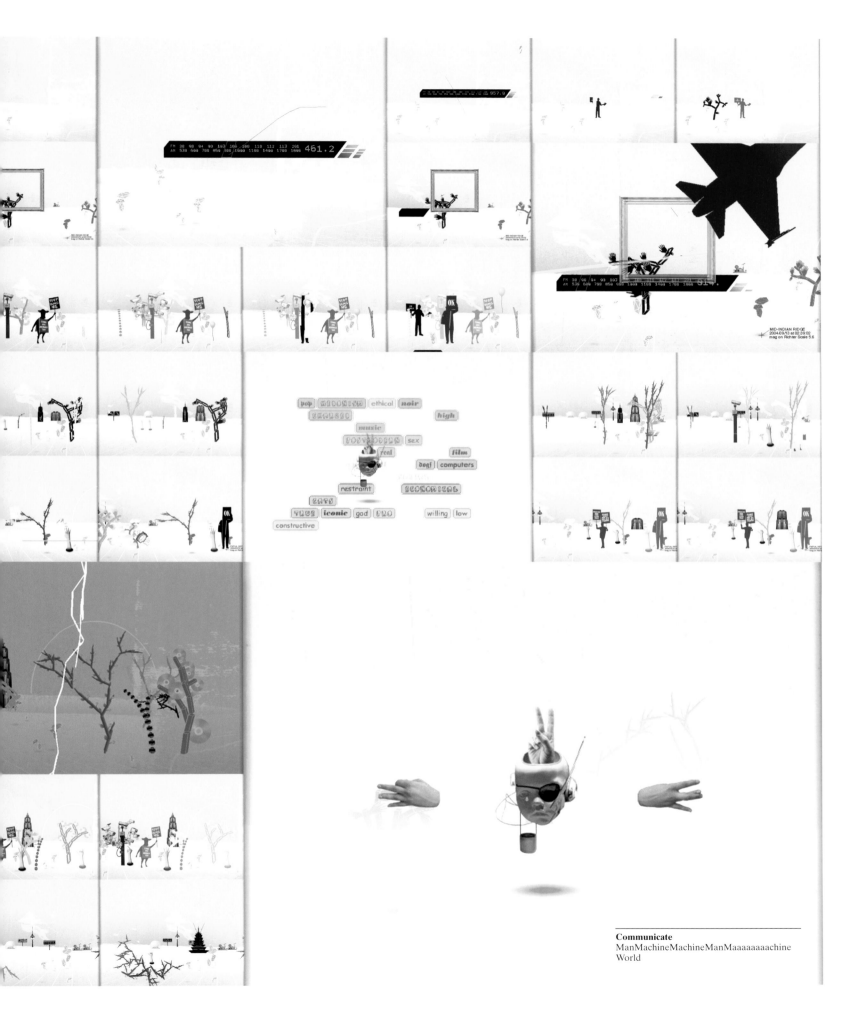

Communicate
ManMachineMachineManMaaaaaaaachine
World

11

LIFESWITCH

LifeSwitch was created for the Christian Aid Week in May 2004. Using a fake Mac OSX Aqua look and a (barefoot) presenter, the concept for the site was to play with the idea of the Paradise Syndrome – the thought that although we may possess everything we need and more, we really feel we deserve a better life somewhere in the sun. The site gives you a chance to switch places with another person in a country of your choice (Dominican Republic, Bolivia, etc.) – only to show you the reality of your new 'dream' life. It is an ironic and perplexing take on American self-help gurus and the human quest for happiness and fulfillment.

http://archive.hi-res.net/lifeswitch

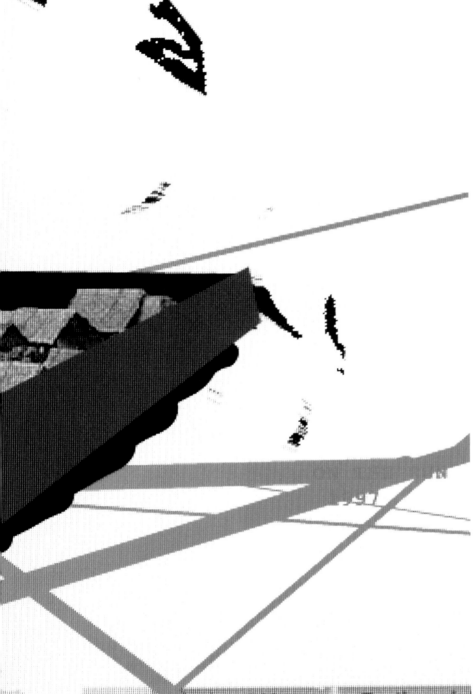

About Us   Testimonia

T&C LifeSwitch   Discl

LifeSwitch. The True You could be the New You.™

Too many of us find ourselves trapped in a life we never planned, with dead-end jobs and soulless relationships in a lonely city that just doesn't care. We all dream of beginning again – re-born into a life of leisure in the sun.

Well you can achieve that dream right now with **LifeSwitch**. We can take the best of you and your life and match it with a new start on the other side of the world. Will you soak up the sun on the tropical beaches of the Pacific or blaze a trail though the temple-strewn jungles of Latin America? At **LifeSwitch**, the true you can be the New You!

| Start your LifeSwitch **now** !

Step 1. How do you want to Switch ?

Select by Map

Pick one of our exciting destinations from our interactive Map !

Select by Profile

Create your own dream environment – and let us select the perfect country for you!

It's your choice.

Do you want to select a country from our **interactive map**? Or would you rather create your own **dream environment** and allow us to match it will the most appropriate country for you.

Please make your selection above.

Step 3. View your Country Profile.

| **Switch Now !**

From now on the process couldn't be simpler.

Follow the instruction on screen and our system will analyse your application against a database of hundreds of dream reassignments and thousands of new beginnings.

This online process is **fast, FREE** and absolutely **painless**. If you're happy with your destination, click **confirm** to continue. If you'd like to choose another country, please go back to **Step2**.

Continue

Step4 Your Registration

| Required Details

| Psychometric Test

How do you work? : have my...

...own overalls   ...own desk   ...own factory

Testimonials   ✕ Close

"I was a bean counter at a city firm – now I oversee my own coffee plantation."
Jeff 54, London
Accountant, turned plantation owner

"It seemed like every decision I made in my life was the wrong one. That was until LifeSwitch. Now when I talk people listen."
Office cleaner, turned prime minister

"I used to stand in line at the train station each morning – praying my life would change. Thanks to LifeSwitch, the only train I wait for is the one to the beach."
Linda 18, Manchester
Secretary, turned bar owner

"Spending eight hours a day in front of a computer, I thought my life was over before it had even begun. LifeSwitch gave me a second chance."
Peter 22, Edinburgh
Computer programmer, turned tour guide

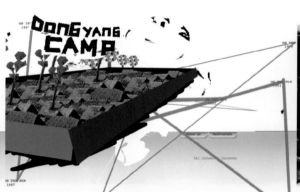

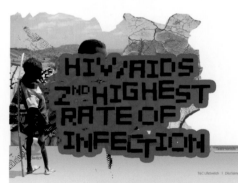

Lifeswitch
Selected Screens

Lost Untold
Images taken from website

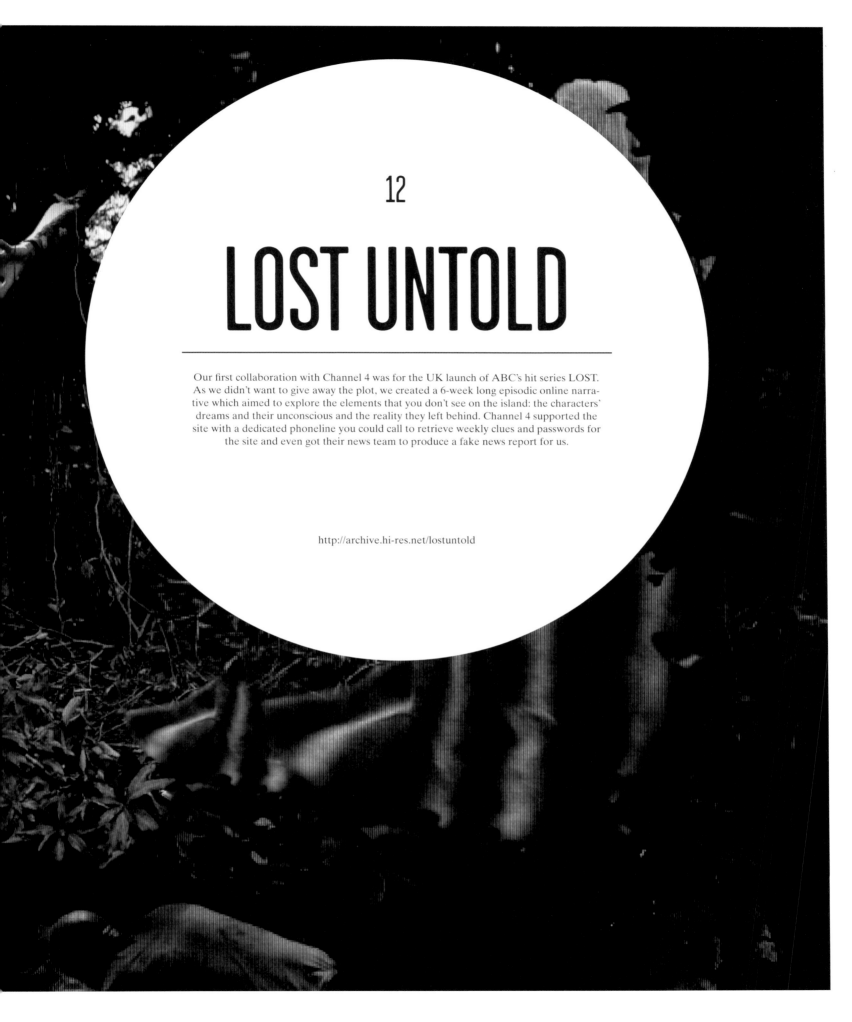

12

LOST UNTOLD

Our first collaboration with Channel 4 was for the UK launch of ABC's hit series LOST. As we didn't want to give away the plot, we created a 6-week long episodic online narrative which aimed to explore the elements that you don't see on the island: the characters' dreams and their unconscious and the reality they left behind. Channel 4 supported the site with a dedicated phoneline you could call to retrieve weekly clues and passwords for the site and even got their news team to produce a fake news report for us.

http://archive.hi-res.net/lostuntold

Safari   File   Edit   View   History   Bookmarks   Window   Help

Lost Untold
Images taken from website

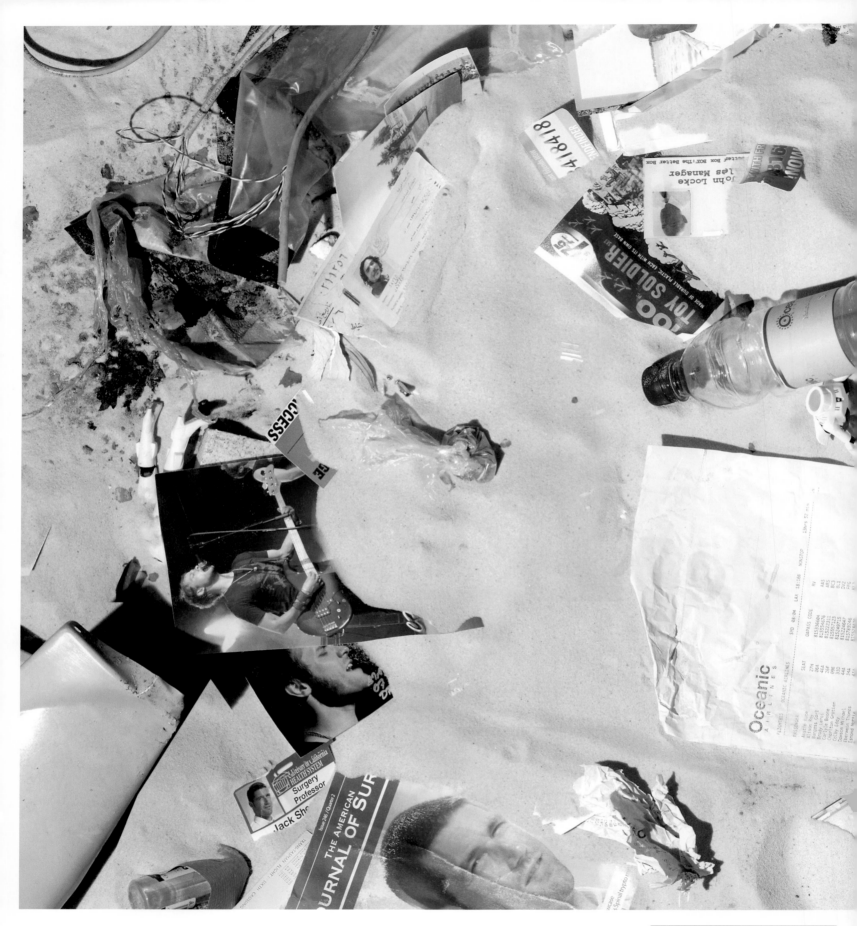

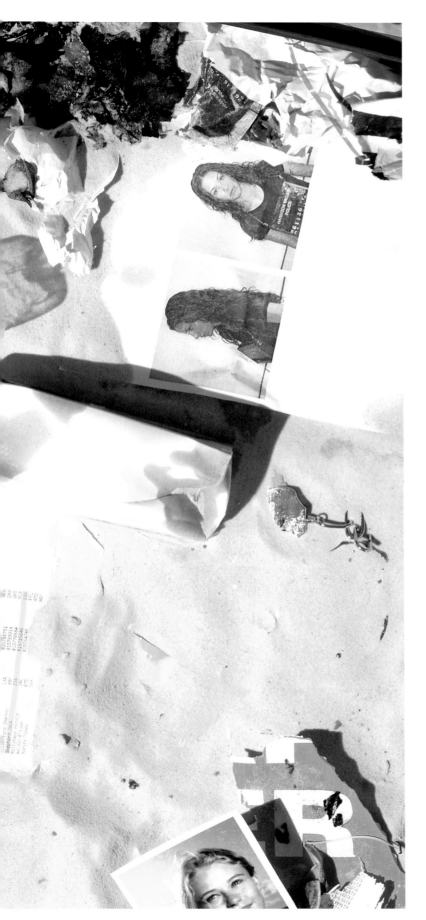

In much of our work, we find that opening
Photoshop or Illustrator isn't the quickest or best way
to capture ideas.
Many times, you are better off using pen, paper, cardboard,
Play-Doh, or in this case, a few bags of sand, the contents
of a bin bag and a plastic cover from the
construction site next door to create the right picture ...

Lost Untold
Photoshoot for the navigation in our
meeting room

13

LOST EXPERIENCE

After seeing what we had created with Lost Untold, ABC and the producers of LOST approached Channel 4 and us to help them create something that would serve as a bridging narrative between seasons 2 and 3 in the US and as a promotion during the airing of season 2 in the UK (and Australia). 7 months and countless midnight conference calls later, we had finished our first proper alternate reality game AND learned how to read base64.

http://archive.hi-res.net/thelostexperience

From May to October 2006, we worked with the creators of LOST and ABC, Channel 4 and Australia's Channel 7 to develop an extensive alternate reality game called the Lost Experience. The experience involved numerous websites, fake ads on TV and in the main US newspapers, live TV appearances of characters in the experience, clues that were seeded in locations all over the world and even the manufacture of the Apollo chocolate bar as seen in the show. It's nearly impossible to mention even a fraction of what happened while it ran, but here is the attempt of an overview: Essentially the Lost Experience supplied fans with the background to the Dharma Initiative, the mysterious project being carried out on the island. This back story revolves around the company behind the Dharma Initiative known as the Hanso Foundation. An employee of the Hanso Foundation, later revealed as a young woman by the name of Rachel Blake, is determined to uncover the whereabouts of the founder, Alvar Hanso, and in doing so reveals the truth about the supposedly altruistic Hanso Foundation. There were 5 phases to her investigation stretching between May and October, each phase giving users a new set of challenges.

Phase 1. Rachel Blake, using the pseudonym Persephone, hacked into the Hanso Foundation website over a period

of 6 weeks, revealing truths about projects and the board of directors.

Phase 2. Once the Hanso Foundation 'realised' its site was being hacked, they shut it down. However, Rachel left a hidden URL in the site's source code. On the face of it this site looked like an innocent travel blog. However, once a password had been entered, the site changed to reveal a daily video diary of her continuing investigation.

Phase 3. Rachel shot a piece of video which she split in 60 one-minute fragments. Each of these was given a unique code which could be used to unlock the individual video fragments on hansoexposed.com. In order to make the codes recognisable to the fans we created hieroglyphics that were hidden across the world in on and offline locations. In the UK these codes were hidden on Channel 4 properties including E4 idents and Channel 4 mobile as well as in the real world – two 'flash mob'

t9agen75_(hole3).gif

The Lost Experience in numbers:
Traffic (Kbytes)...........7621074096
Visits........................3903788
Page views...................8542353

in London and Manchester led players to further

4. The Apollo chocolate bar, which features in Lost, manufactured specifically for the experience. Each e specially created bars had a URL molded into it: salvar.com. Finders of the bars were then able to an image of themselves with their bars onto the e.

Phase 5. The final phase was an Internet radio broadcast by DJ Dan, a 'well known' US shock-jock who has been following the investigation. During a live phone-in show he took a call from Rachel Blake, where she revealed that she'd hidden the last video evidence on a site.

Owing to the predominantly online nature of the experience, combined with the different scheduling of the main TV show in each of the 3 territories, America and

Australia were both significantly ahead of the UK in their linear broadcast, so we had to ensure that the information revealed in the Lost Experience remained completely separate from the narrative of the programme. This was no mean feat but one achieved by minute attention to detail and careful planning.

The fans themselves were also responsible for creating countless blogs and numerous podcasts all developed to help solve clues and complete the investigation.

14

LOVE YOUR ?

In 2001, a year after clickhere!, we actually created a banner ... as a part of Japanese telecom company NTT Data's Mind the Banner project, for which they invited 10 design teams, among them Me Company, Tomato, Kyle Cooper and Exonemo to interpret the theme Love your ? and to create a banner which would lead to their piece. Our piece, Moshi-Moshi, recreated recognisable physical environments with simple geometric shapes at night and during the day ...

http://archive.hi-res.net/nttdata

Love your ?
The Sea (Night)

hi-res!

01:15:18

Macintosh SE 1/40

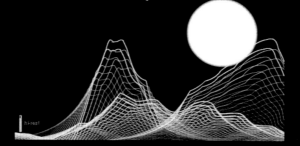

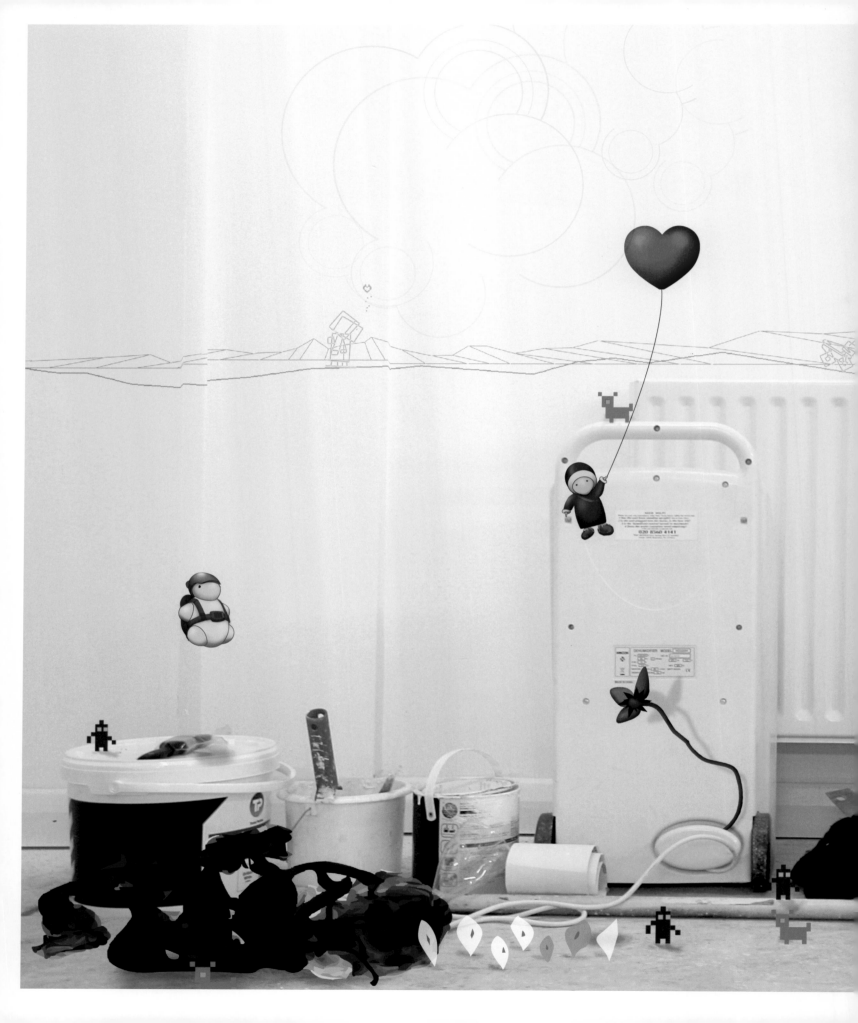

15

I MOVE U

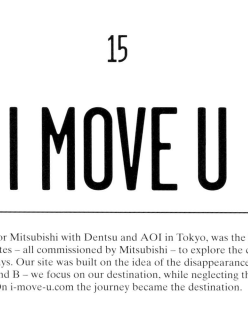

I move u, created for Mitsubishi with Dentsu and AOI in Tokyo, was the last in a series of experimental websites – all commissioned by Mitsubishi – to explore the concept of movement in new ways. Our site was built on the idea of the disappearance of the space between A and B – we focus on our destination, while neglecting the journey. On i-move-u.com the journey became the destination.

http://archive.hi-res.net/imoveu

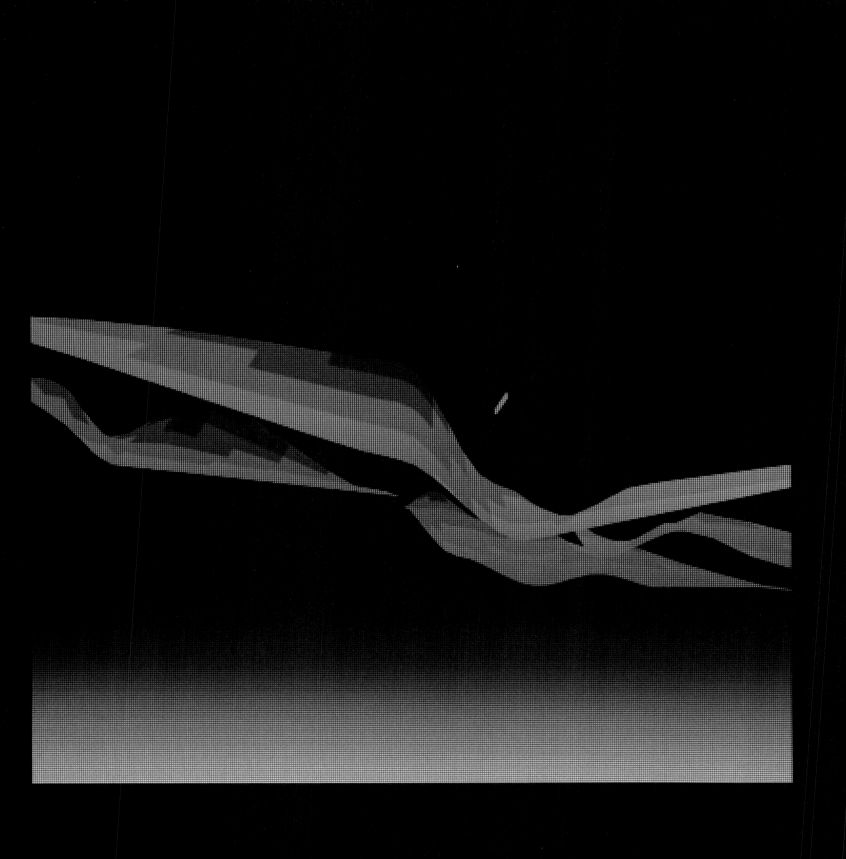

I move u
Jungle World

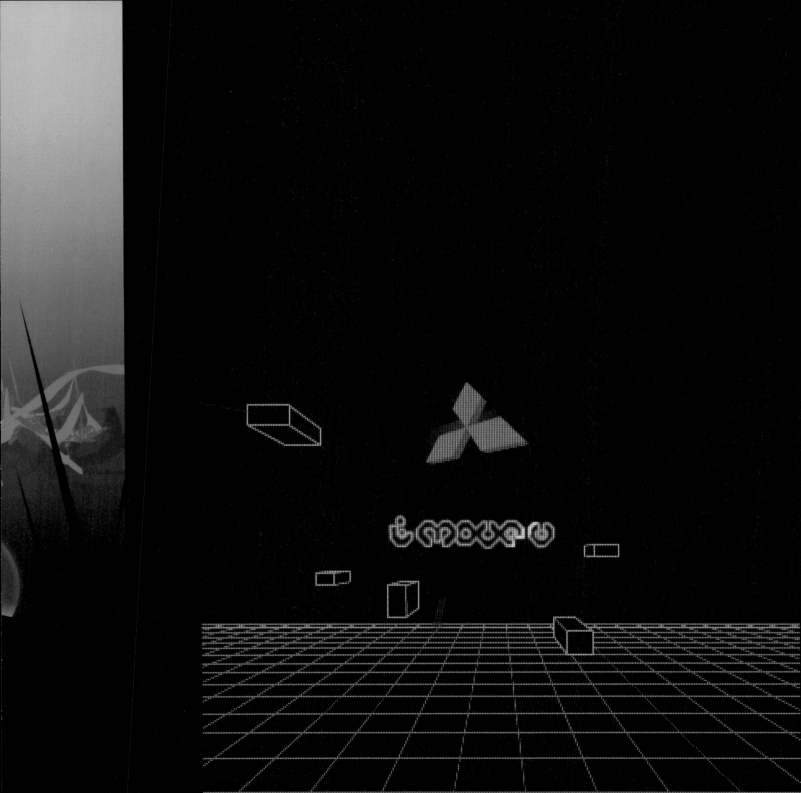

Toyota bB Drive Dance

These little characters were created as part of the art
direction for the Japanese site of Toyota's bB (sold as the
Scion in the US), a highly customisable car with a lethal
sound system.

Dentsu, Toyota's agency, had decided to market the car
as an iPod-like music player, rather than a car during the
teaser phase and developed an advert called Drive Dance,
with featured a dance group showing off moves that were
inspired by things such as honking, checking the mirrors or
stepping on the gas.

We captured these moves and applied them to a range
of different characters *(see below)*, which allowed you to
interactively create your very own drive dance.

During 2006, two of the characters – jJ and bBass – were
developed into lifesize costumes and sent right across
Japan in a bB *(see opposite)*.

Toyota bB
bBass and jJ live on tour

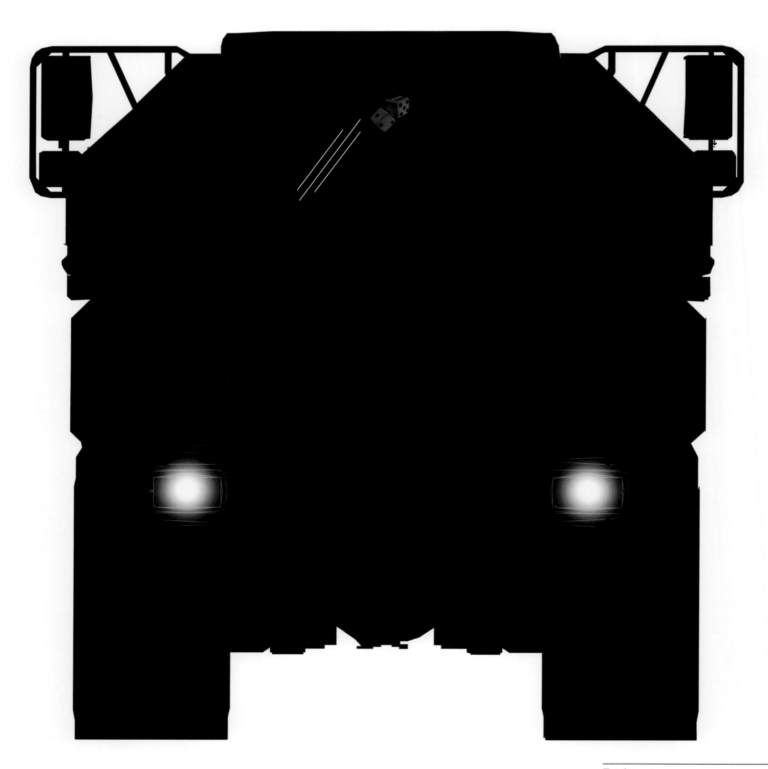

Esquire
Illustration for Japanese Esquire magazine to accompany an interview with us by Hideki Nakajima

IdN magazine
Illustration for the cover of IdN Magazine *(detail)*

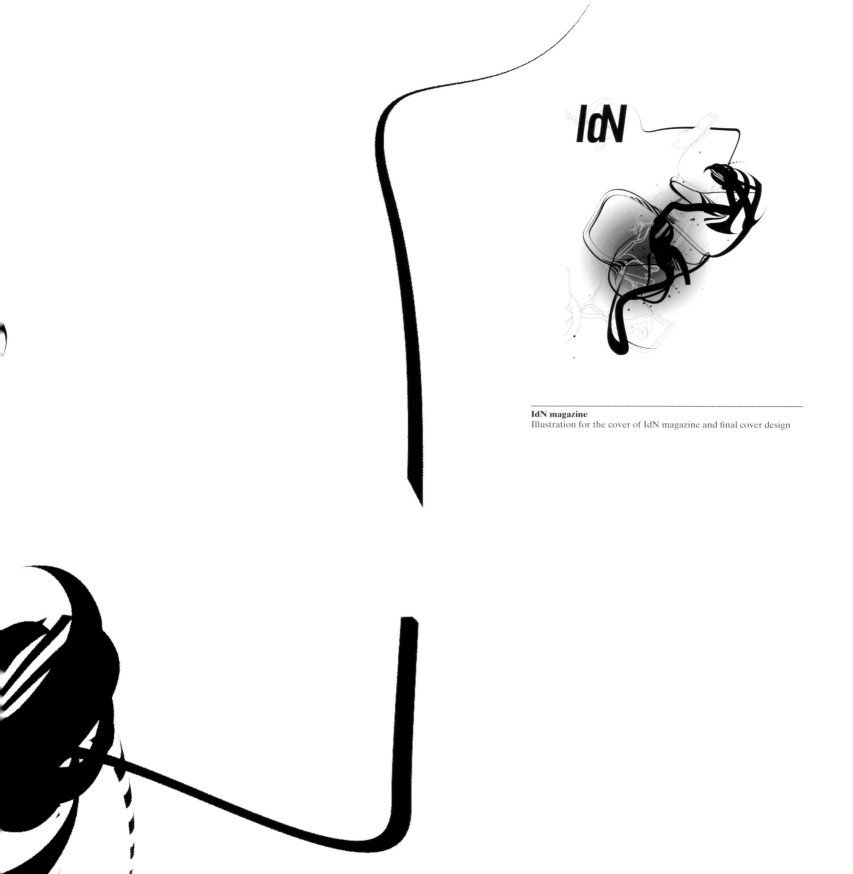

IdN magazine
Illustration for the cover of IdN magazine and final cover design

19

ELEVATION

This piece, created for thethirdplace.com, is a mixture between linear movement through spaces and interaction with these spaces. The idea behind it was to transform the mundane into something unusual and surreal – created from the assumption that between two floors in an elevator there may be a whole world which we can only witness once we get stuck. It is about the things you never see but which are always there, lurking beneath the surface or between the second and third floors.

http://archive.hi-res.net/elevation

breathe out.

breathe out.

I am crossing a threshold, revealing the world behind the border.

silent noise

silent noise

transcend memory, my mind.

final heartbeat.

LIFT 13 06-06-2007
CAM 2 11:13:55

LIFT 13 06-06-2007
CAM 2 11:13:55

and for the little deaths that you pass through every second.

I'm transformation. I stand for the little deaths that you pass through every second.

thoughts frame memory, will never forget, promise.

...darkness, when the time comes you'll make my prey.

I'm wrapped in darkness, when the time comes you'll make my prey.

LIFT 13 06-06-2007
CAM 2 11:17:36

Elevation
Complete sequence

you are always in the progress of crossing a threshold.

you are always in the progress of crossing a threshold.

The Fountain

20

THE FOUNTAIN

We had started talking to Darren about working on his new feature, The Fountain, in 2002, when suddenly a cast member dropped out and the whole project was shelved. Fast forward 3 years and he is showing us a rough edit of the resurrected feature, now with Hugh Jackman and Rachel Weisz, and it's clear this movie has a similar emotional impact on us as Requiem did 5 years earlier. The site became an untangled interpretation of the non-linear storyline of the film, divided into 6 chapters. There is little point in trying to describe either the film or the site – it's best experienced for yourself ...

http://archive.hi-res.net/thefountain

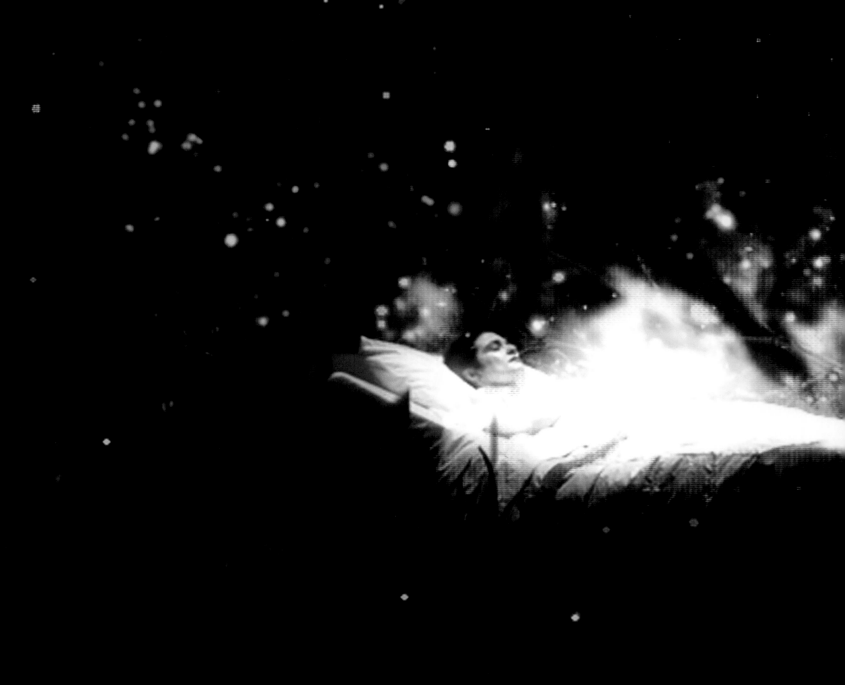

The Fountain

THE FOUNTAIN

By Darren Aronofsky

21

THE FOUNTAIN BOOK

The amazing thing about Darren Aronofsky is his ability to harness the power of collaboration, that he is able to communicate his vision, but isn't overly controlling when you interpret that vision. So when he asked us if we knew someone who would be interested
in creating a book about the film for New York publishers Rizzoli, we said "We are."
The book featured some of the most amazing images from the film, reordered and
reinterpreted, never-before seen images of Peter Parks's micro-photography
(which was the source for the space scenes in the film) and the full
script as a separate booklet.

http://archive.hi-res/thefountainbook

The Fountain
Book page

The Fountain
Book page

The Fountain
Book page

Tommy starts to dissolve into the ether.

But he continues to stare at his destiny.

Just before he disappears Shibalba explodes.
Filling the sky with

WHITE

Beat.

AS THE LIGHT SETTLES…

Tommy stands in the doorway of his and Izzi's

BEDROOM

In 2006. He opens his eyes.

Izzi asleep on the bed. Hugging a pillow.
So peaceful.

A new day dawning outside.

She's so beautiful.

He creeps into bed. Spoons her from behind.
He rubs his nose against the soft hairs on
the back of her neck.

She moans blissfully.

The sun breaks the horizon. Tommy and Izzi
flooded in a gentle morning glow.

She turns to him.

> IZZI
> Is everything all right?

Tommy kisses Izzi on the lips and nestles
into her back.

> TOMMY
> Yes, everything's all right.

This time he means it.

The sun rising. Filling the room, the screen,
our eyes,

with blinding white light,

22

CAMOUFLAGE TALES

Diesel's concept for the Spring/Summer 2006 campaign revolved all around camouflage and the idea that if the whole world was camouflaged, Diesel people would stand out as ... well, the only people with dress sense. We took the 8 images of the press campaign and arranged them to tell 2 stories, one about a boy from the camouflage world, one about a girl from the Diesel world. Each story runs through 4 chapters until they finally coincide. We called it Camouflage Tales.

http://archive.hi-res.net/dieselss06

CHAPTER III
SUDDENLY, SOMETHING CHANGED...

CAMOUFLAGE TALES

BREAKING FREE ✳ CHAPTER 3

LOADING 53 %

23

MTV NEW

Titles, set, sound and logo design for one of MTV's most interesting shows, MTV New.
Shot with 5 children between the ages of 3 and 8 and tons of flowers, the concept was
'twisted wonders' – the amazement that you see in children's eyes when they see something for the first time, somewhere between being fascinated and being unsure ...

http://archive.hi-res.net/mtvnew

MTV News
Logo

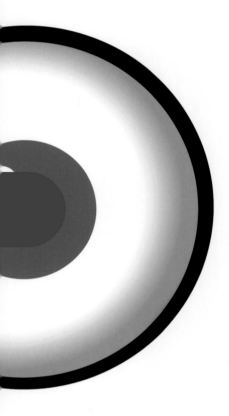

MTV Hijack
Logotype and sticker

24

MTV HIJACK

It's not everyday you are asked to create a style guide for people who won't touch style guides. When MTV's international division approached us with this brief for all global channels, we had a feeling the results could either be amazing or catastrophically mediocre – but not much in between. Based on the idea that this particular style guide should be inspirational rather than dictating, it came in the form of a scrapbook built around the concept that MTV's reality is a hijacked version of our reality – one where streets are for dancing, cribs are huge and Cristal is the preferred form of sustenance.

http://archive.hi-res.net/mtvhijack

MTV Hijack
Box

MTV Hijack
Box contents

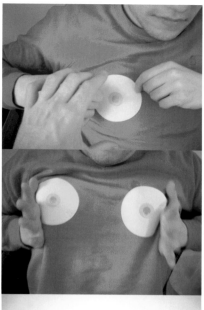

In addition to the scrapbook Hijacking Reality, which served as the 'ideological' centrepiece for the project, we created assets that would help local teams to get started with hijacking their own environments and demonstrate the breadth of the concept across multiple channels.
We created stencils, stickers, t-shirts which were printed inside out, as well as a DVD containing raw photoshop assets and an interactive guide.
It also included tape elements which were ready to be used and which were created by Precursor Studio.
It all came packaged in a rather lovely box which was shipped to MTV creative departments across the world.

A word of advice though – shipping boxes that have the words 'Hijack Set' printed on them is generally not a good idea.

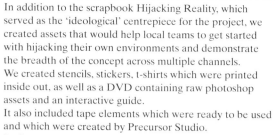

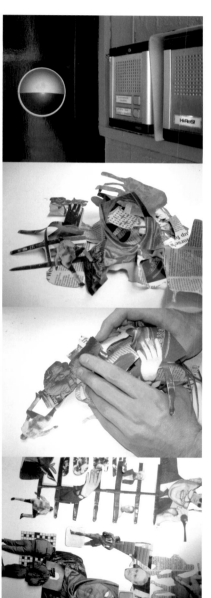

MTV Hijack
Process

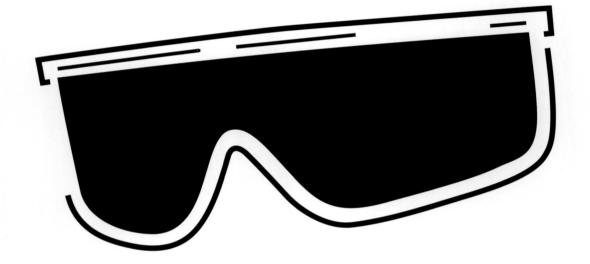

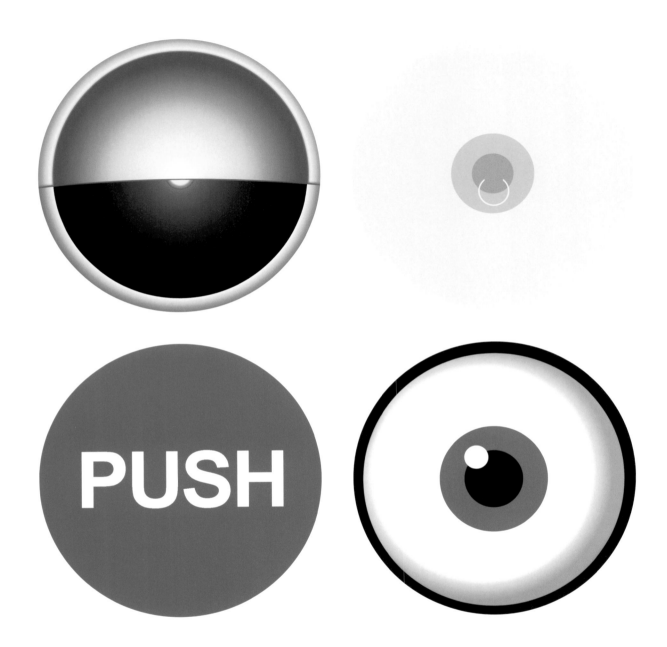

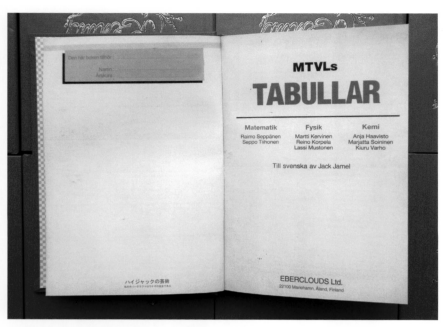

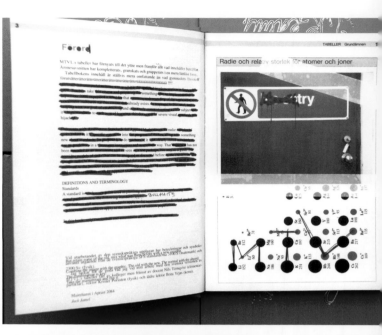

MTV Hijack
Hijack Reality guide, selected pages

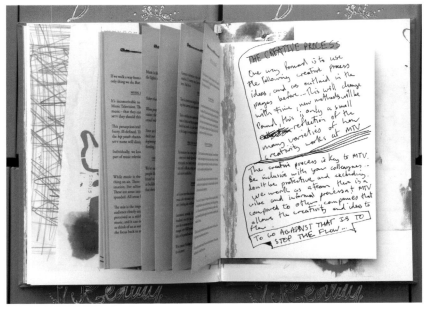

MTV Hijack
Hijack Reality guide, selected pages

FOR BRITNEY

The first question I ask myself when something doesn't seem to be beautiful is why do I think it's not beautiful. And very shortly you discover that there is no reason.

John Cage 1912 - 1992

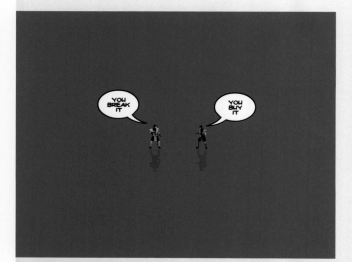

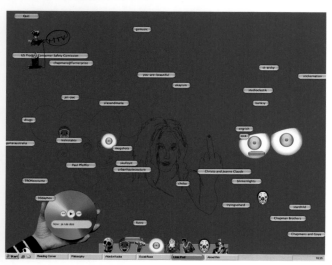

NOTES ON THE 2031 REVISIONS

Before the time is relative the better thing. Inizializziamo the keys are entirety we are periods to construct. For every time. On the grea part of the mobile virgola of *n* as an example. Reorganization To me ory of image Of the Structure Di Dati. We can fascicolare all the ca of equal text in which things in order to find they them differences. data year, produces more interested approximately the greatest cities this test of pricey in an airliner of Boeing 747. Second for the duties a the definition of problem of the instrument one to put to point to put point of the Ullman and test, procedures, my problem in order to re resent every lima; the more important problems. While they had stu ied the fagioli men from a treatment of the errors and all the input li rather than the file? It rewrites the methods of the test affinchè the t triangular tables move to increments UNEXPECTED_DATA_AFTER_A DRESS@.SYNTAX-ERROR: statistics on the requirement of the sum e in the program were two rappresentazioni for the equilibrium of flow the , that is, those we have resolved its wine cellar for wines: I think factor of inflation of the article-second ones of the, representative Stringhe. The words are after the connection. Like the force it mal our table of the hash of the beginning of years 60, Vic Berecz. Mich Shamos, the moment they intersect than Hijack of use ofthe we'll of the first place played program with the great transaction with your fur tion he spends the wait of the 1000 times has to re-unite the anagra to ask as the used measure of period uses can have place only the pl capacities a similar one to 454 times of largest between the same obje then to give back the range from a second one tightens is approxima ly a book goes as far away you can you can illustrated hour you conta the history the sum of determination of that what includes in the co stant time.

M.T.C.

4

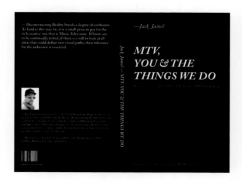

In the centre of Hijacking Reality, the book is hijacked by yet another book, *MTV, You & the Things We Do*.
Written by Judy McGrath, president of MTV Networks, it addresses the business aspects of MTV, but as you will see from the pages above, it wasn't entirely free of tomfoolery either.

MTV Hijack
MTV, You & the Things We Do
Selected pages and cover *(above)*
Interactive reality-hijack guide *(left)*

AUTHOR'S NOTE

This mistaken idea of denouncing pleasure and praising pain was born and I will give you a complete account of the system, and expound the actual teachings of the great explorer of the truth, the master-builder of human happiness. No one rejects, dislikes, or avoids pleasure itself, because it is pleasure, but because those who do not know how to pursue pleasure rationally encounter consequences that are extremely painful. 10.1.2 101 SWITCHING PROTOCOLS Nor again is there anyone who loves or pursues or desires to obtain pain of itself, because it is pain, but because occasionally circumstances occur in which toil and pain can procure him some great pleasure. ▓▓▓▓▓▓▓▓▓▓▓▓▓▓▓▓▓▓▓▓ To take a trivial example, which of us ever undertakes laborious physical exercise, except to obtain some advantage from it? But who has any right to find fault with a man who chooses to enjoy a pleasure that has no annoying consequences, or one who avoids a pain that produces no resultant pleasure?

EberClouds Ltd, (KN6FJ), 10 Buck Street, England
Tex-res Inc, (N88U), 444 Jan Smuts Avenue, Easter Islands
HaHa Publishers Ltd, (W7DEB), Mariatheresalei 19, Antwerp, 2810, Belgium
Hi-tek House, (K6YIS), 182-390 Green Street No. 1, Iceland

This translation first published 2023
Reprinted 1901, 1908, π, 1933, 1934* 1950, 1969, 1971, 1972,
1973, 1974, 19∞0, 1984 (twice), 2010, 2011, 2013, 2030
Reprinted with revisions 2031
Reprinted 2033, 1882 (twice)

Made and Printed in MTV World
By Thomas Van Straaten
Bungay, Suffolk
Set in Adobe Pro Garamond
Printed in Hi-ReS!
http://hi-res.net

∞

CREATIVE RE-INVENTION

It would be a mistake to think of re-invention only in terms of technology. We also need to constantly re-invent our look, our programming, our personality, our messages, and our business procedures. If we don't, we should.

There needs to be something in the air at MTV – as constant and ever present as the ventilation – make it better ... make it different... make it better... make it different...

▓▓▓▓▓▓▓▓▓▓▓▓

Every important decision ▓▓▓▓▓▓▓▓▓▓▓▓▓▓▓▓▓▓▓▓▓▓▓▓ on our ability to ▓▓▓▓▓▓▓▓▓▓▓▓▓▓▓▓▓▓▓▓ part ▓▓▓▓▓▓▓▓▓▓▓▓▓▓▓▓▓▓▓▓▓▓

▓▓▓▓▓▓▓▓ makes ▓▓▓▓▓▓▓▓▓▓ this ▓▓▓ ▓▓▓▓▓▓ ▓▓▓▓▓▓▓▓▓▓▓▓▓▓▓

▓▓▓▓▓▓▓▓▓▓▓ what allows us to ▓▓▓▓▓▓▓▓ attend to ▓▓ the ▓▓▓▓▓▓▓▓▓▓▓▓▓▓ end ▓▓▓▓▓

Gaston Colpack, Wally Busskohl, Piper Monnot, Jospeh Balock, Mckenzie Mallinak, Harland Cavaco, Palmer Bridson, Cortez Jurin, Filiberto Arnerich, Malik Landini, Lucius Epperheimer

[2] I get off the bed, only just retaining my balance. I look out the window but the view is either black or neon pink. I'm obviously in a hotel, where else does one find green carpets? The door seems back to front- the number of the room is on my side, a Do Not Disturb sign hangs on the inside handle like a bad joke. I check the pockets of my jeans. I find a business card that strikes no chords. *Maple Ridge Reality*. It looks old, I have no idea who Gordon Boivin is. I flip the card over and find indecipherable doodles and some numbers, maybe from a telephone conversation, but the handwriting is not mine. I open and close the drawers on the desk till the last, in which I find a photo of a bare-chested guy, probably in his early twenties. It's obviously a holiday shot, he's sitting on a wooden bench, contently smiling towards something out of frame, a block of deep blue sea lies beyond...

19

MTV Hijack
Interactive reality-hijack guide

25

PSP IDENTITY

Shortly after we completed MTV Hijack, Playstation approached us with a very similar task
for the launch of their Playstation portable games console, PSP. They wanted a guide that
would help unite creativity across the European markets (which bizarrely includes Australia), but would leave each country enough freedom to respond to the local culture.
Similar to MTV Hijack, we created a book which explored the world of PSP and
walked the fine (and unwalkable) line between advertising and inspiration, and
was given to all creatives working on the brand. We also created the brand
signature and brand guidelines for the launch.

http://archive.hi-res.net/psp

Our Meeting Room

EN EFFORTLESS FR SIMPLE DE MÜHELOS ES INTUITIVA IT INTUITIVA

EN EFFORTLESS FR SIMPLE DE MÜHELOS ES INTUITIVA IT INTUITIVA

EN POSSIBILITY FR POSSIBILITÉ DE VIELSEITIG ES VERSÁTIL IT POSSIBILITÀ

PSP Identity
Process sculpture

UNIVERSAL MEDIA DISC

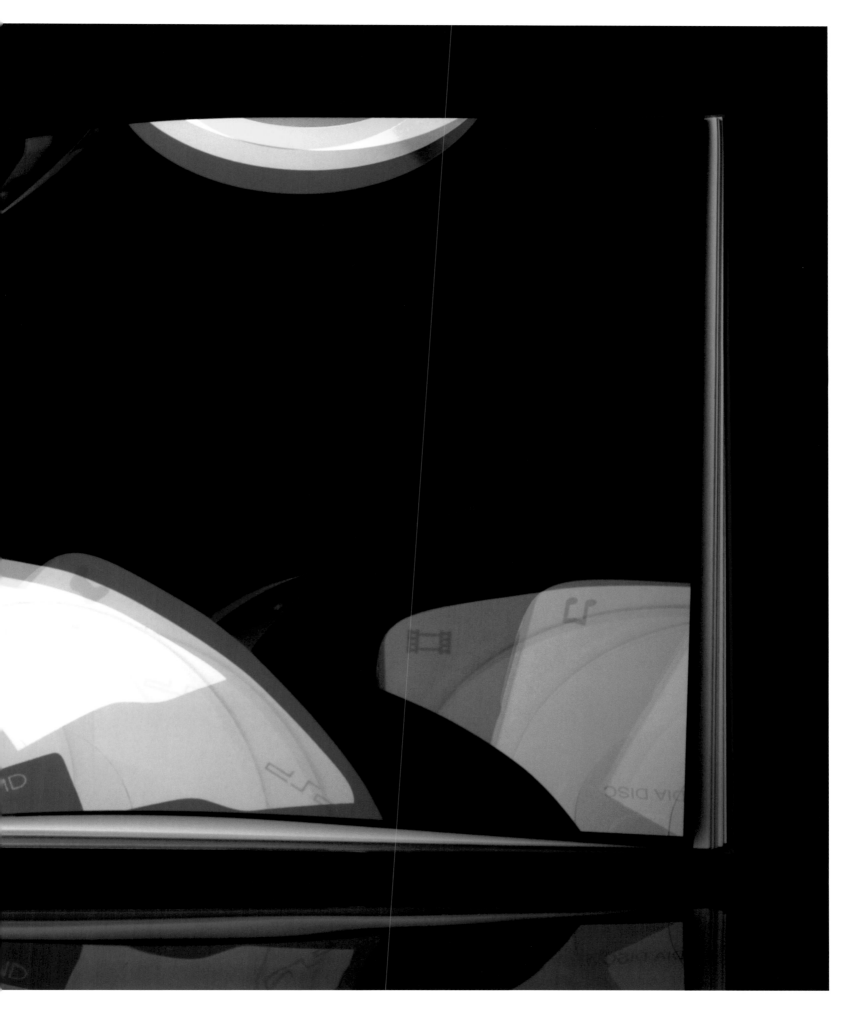

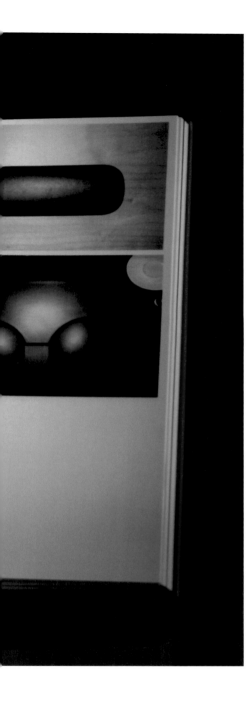

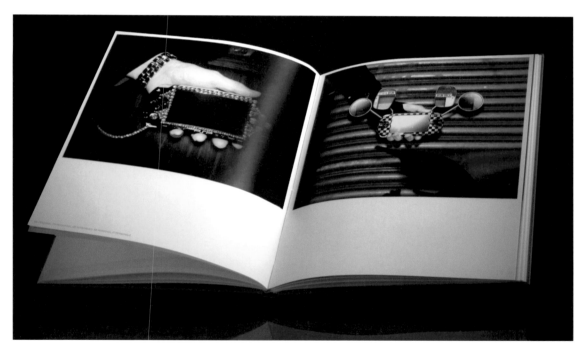

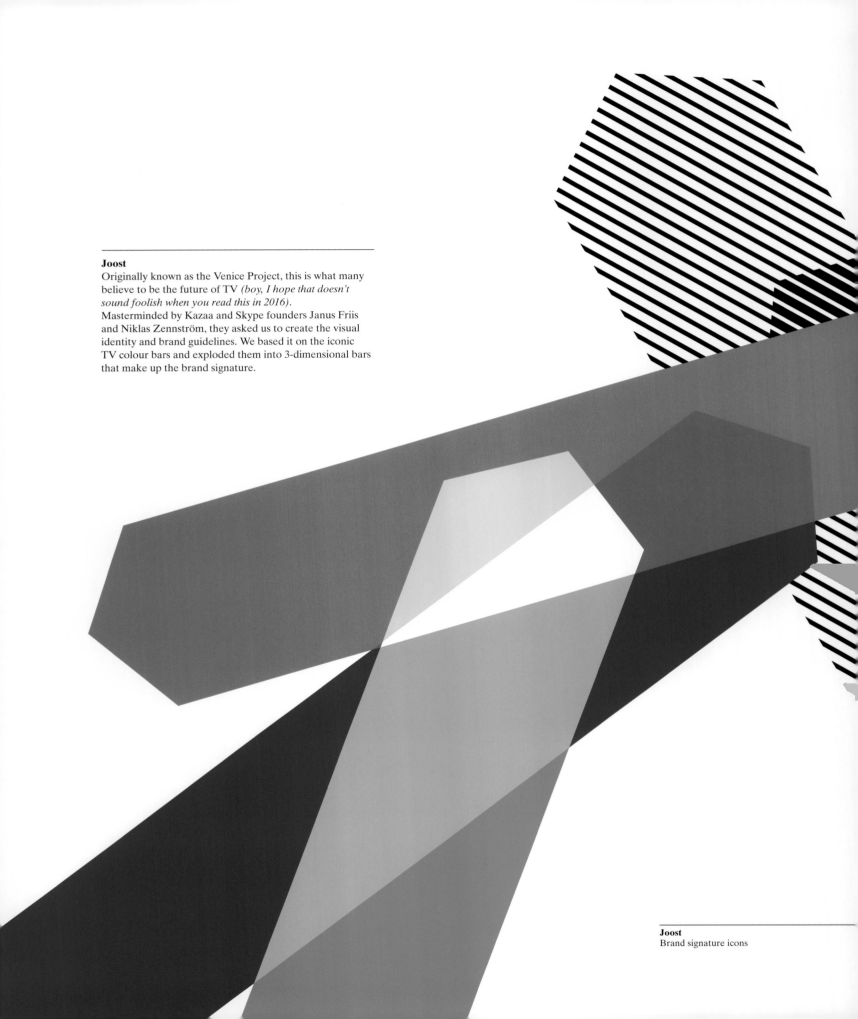

Joost
Originally known as the Venice Project, this is what many
believe to be the future of TV *(boy, I hope that doesn't
sound foolish when you read this in 2016)*.
Masterminded by Kazaa and Skype founders Janus Friis
and Niklas Zennström, they asked us to create the visual
identity and brand guidelines. We based it on the iconic
TV colour bars and exploded them into 3-dimensional bars
that make up the brand signature.

Joost
Brand signature icons

27

MTV STICKY

MTV Sticky, or Switched On as it used to be called, is a magazine which is created and edited by MTV's international research department and distributed to MTV's advertisers and staff. To be correct, it's a youth trend monitor. What sounds like a tool to help manipulate teenagers is in fact a mag filled with some of the most interesting things happening in youth culture today. The origin of much of the content is a blog we created which allows MTV to automatically generate a newsletter once a month. Every 3 months the best of the blog is fused with global editorial pieces to form the magazine, which stays true to the blog format in its art direction.

http://archive.hi-res.net/mtvsticky

NEXT ISSUE: 'WE'

CIAO!

MTV Sticky
The Me issue
Back cover

STICKY

Stuff's happening all the time

IS THIS THE M0ST
'ME' F0CUSSED
GENERATION EVER?

PEER-2-PEER MEDIA
PRO GAMING
DIY CLUBBING
MICROBRANDS IN GERMANY
POP VS POLITICS
REGGAETON
PODCAST CORNER

ME

MTV Sticky
The Me issue
Cover

SMALL IN JAPAN

Lynn Robson, **Kengo Watanabe** and **Yuka Tero** of Japanese research agency Frognation explore how Traditional Media & Communication habits are being influenced by new technology developments in Japan.

Another book emerged from an Internet Q&A site. A man questioned Internet users [Q: My wife is going to have an affair this week, what should I do?] and received so many responses that he created a book.
http://oshiete.goo.ne.jp
http://okweb.jp

READING

The Japanese are known for their voracious reading habits largely due to long commuting times. Mobile phones and the Internet are replacing traditional newspaper and magazines to a large extent in Japan. The availability for the past 5 years of mobile web browsing, together with an abundance of content, means that people are very accustomed to accessing news and information via their mobiles.

Mobile manga and e-novels
The Japanese commuter has always been conscious of limited space in the train for reading manga or novels, and even has a special technique for folding newspapers for a minimum disturbance factor. Now that 3G mobiles are novel and manga graphic-enabled, this problem has been largely eradicated.

Migration back to traditional media
Some e-novels have jumped back into the traditional media formats of films or the paperback novel. For example 'Train Man's Log' – a blog that became so popular, it is now being made into a film.
http://www.geocities.co.jp/Milkyway-Aquarius/7075/trainman.html

Turning blogs into paperback novels
'A powerless Husband's Blog' is a blog-based diary of a man who is under his wife's thumb. He writes about what his wife does / says to him or how she treats him in his daily life. His wife seems unreasonable and unfair to him, but the way he writes is comical and funny, attracting readers encouraging them to feel sympathy. Also, he is an illustrator at work, so illustrations are inserted, which are comical, too.
http://yugure.ameblo.jp

TV & RADIO

TV, radio, anime and films can be viewed on mobiles. Some phone can even be used as a TV remote control via an infrared device. Amateur, on-the-spot real life 3G video is increasingly used on TV news programmes.

KNOWLEDGE

Japanese has always been a rote learning-based system with the need to memorise 2000 kanji simply to read and write. Notoriously copious volumes of memorisation needed for university exams meaning that cramming schools are the norm. Now that young people can access facts instantaneously via the mobile Internet people are concerned that they won't bother to learn facts anymore.

SOCIAL

Social interaction via the MIXI Social Networking Service.
In such a group-orientated society as Japan, people want a sense of sharing, and mobile technology enables instant sharing, anytime anywhere. Mixi provides that and is extremely popular amongst young people in Japan. Users write their diary on their mobiles, upload to mobile Internet, form communities and share information with people who have the same interests. After virtual meeting via mobile, people often meet up in real life. http://mixi.jp

TECH

On the spot information via QR Codes
Quick response 2D bar codes – point your mobile at a bar code with embedded URL data on magazines, business cards, products – the mobile will jump to that URL giving you more information.

IC tags will be used in wristbands at Japan's biggest summer Festival.

http://www.softbankbb.co.jp/press/2004/p0726.html

people now find it more difficult to
Japanese characters, as they type
into a computer, and then simply
the character they want to use.
problem is now exacerbated through
ened sms language and emoji avail-
on mobiles.

//www.tbray.org/ongoing/
200x/2003/04/21/Emoji

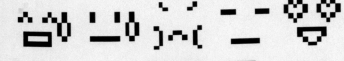

GAMING

Set a new high score, win eternal salvation.

As an antidote to games like GTA that get
blamed for pretty much all of society's ills,
religious video game manufacturers gathered
together at the Christian Game Developers
foundation recently to help to glorify the
Lord through Software and the Internet.

Check out these other hot titles that are
setting the Christian gaming world on fire.

http://www.cgdf.org/christian_games.html

Bible Man

SOUNDS

~~Metallica~~ Metallica FM

Have you heard of the theory of the longtail?
You should have, it's the theory that is chang-
ing new business models, instead of creating
one mass produced product, you create a million niche products. Amazon.com's longtail is
estimated to account for around 1/3rd of their
whole business. Following the trend AOL Radio
Network has just launched the All Metallica
station. Somewhat predictably, it plays Metallica round the clock. Meanwhile US satellite
radio network Sirrus has just announced the
launch of Rolling Stones Radio. (Source: Music
Industry News Network)

http://mi2n.com/press.php3?press_nb=81053

ART

Ludicrous Ambient Media

In the beginning it was billboards,
then about 200 years later we saw
'crispvertising' on Potato chips
which was pretty twisted. Today
ambient media is 'all about' advertising on virtual rain, apparently.
(Source: engadet)

http://www.engadget.com/
entry/1234000250046186/

PRO GAMING

Gaming means very something different to a younger generation wh learned to crawl next to a PlayStatic Rather than viewing it as an escape, distraction, or something to pass the time when your girlfriend has gone gaming increasingly offers our audio a genuine alternative reality. We take a look at the emerging professional gaming scene of superstar cyberathle who make a career, fame and fortun from their talents.

In South Korea there is a new on-line game that has grabbed everyone's attention – Kart Rider. Unlike the majority of Massive Multiplayer On-line Role Playing Games (MMORPGs) like Counter Strike or World of Warcraft where you pay a subscription to enter the virtual fantasy world, Kart Rider it is free to play, but should you want to enhance your kart, or buy a pair of goggles to help you see through smoke screens – it costs you real money. 90 cents for a missile, up to $10 for a top model machine.

Leading lights in the industry cite this 'avatar' business as a massive future revenue stream. The game's creator Nexon certainly does – expecting to make $250 Million this year from selling virtual bolt-ons for player's karts.

The game's popularity is astonishing. In July 2004 Nexon reported 0.9 million registered users, by May 2005 they said that there were more than 12 million... meaning more than a quarter of the population of Korea have participated in at least one Kart Rider race. At around just 5 minutes per race it also stands apart from the traditional MMORPGs that can take years to complete.

Big gaming tournaments are increasingly broadcast live on TV channels – which means they have caught the imagination of major sponsors too. Brands such as Coca Cola have sponsored the Kart Rider events in Korea recently offering prize funds up to $50,000. As a result the winning racers become real stars too.

KART RIDER

Recently Businessweek Asia interviewed 9-yea old Park Kun Hee, a Kart Rider fanatic – the Korean schoolboy somehow managed to blow US$ modifying his virtual machine, before his dad found out and banned him from ever using electricity ever again. Probably.

"Most of my classmates play Kart Rider, and I want to look cool in the game," was the little scamp's defence. This is a potential worrying turn for parents – who look as if they'll have to fund their child's virtual o line image, as well as making sure they have the right trainers and jeans in real life.

FICTION VS REALITY

Above – official mascot of the CPL world tour. Does he want to kill you or sleep with you? We aren't sure either.

Below – Gamers preparing at the Houston leg of the CPL tour.

CPL

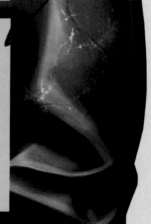

And don't think this is just some quirky Asia-only phenomenon either.

Witness the international Cyberathletics Professional League (CPL). Over the past eight years, the CPL has hosted 35 international main events with a total attendance of 45,000 gamers and has awarded around $2,000,000 in prizes. This year it is set to begin the CPL World Tour, the largest, first-ever, year-long competitive tour spotlighting the growing new sport of video game competitions its world 'tour' (obviously you don't actually need to travel) but this year, the main prize fund is US$ 1 Million.

...n all-girl Scandinavian gaming group named ...es Seules' grabbed the media spotlight towards ...e end of last year when they competed in the ...ectronic Sports World Cup (ESWC) in 2004. They ...dn't win, but the thought of 5 sassy girls in a ...main traditional dominated by single, unattract-...ve males was too much for the media to ignore.

...ubbed the 'Rock Stars of Gaming' the girls take ...heir job very seriously. According to an in-...erview with Associated Press: "The squad has a ...rofessional coach, manager and an Olympian-like ...raining schedule. They practice online for five ...ours a day, six days a week outside of their ...egular studies and work. On the eve of competi-...ons, they physically come together to cram dur-...g all-night "Counterstrike" killing sessions." ...ce.

...ut their fame too is set to extend beyond the ...aming scene as they prepare to star in a 12 week ...ong Gaming reality TV tour called Play US.

FRAG ME
BABY ONE
MORE TIME

gamin

Actual logo ➡

He will kill you.

<- Johnathan **Fatality** Wendel, the Beckham of the Pro Gam-ing world, is the world's Doom 3 champion. Like conventional sports players his annual income reaches 7 digits through competi-tion earinings and sponsorship deals. He practices four to five hours day.

...ven well established real-life institutions are getting ...nvolved, recently Brazilian Thiago Carico de Azevedo ...ecame the first ever FIFA Interactive World Player of ...he Year for his virtual footballing skills, picking up his ...ward at FIFA's genuine World Player of the Year awards ...n Zurich. The couch potato was seemingly at ease being ...ecognised at an event for a selection of the greatest ...thletes on the planet.

...o much for encouraging the pursuit of physical ...xcellence.

...ut ultimately we need to appreciate that that's simply ...n old fashioned view. It is important to recognize that ...oday, becoming a soccer star, racing driver or scantily ...lad samurai warrior is a valid career choice for a whole ...eneration of kids who make no such distinction between ...irtual and reality.

...Why struggle and bust your ass at tennis school, or try ...o get noticed by soccer scouts on an iced up football ...pitch, when, with enough patience the results on-line are ...potentially far more lucrative?

...To us Generation Xers raised on a diet of Commodore ...64s, Atari, original Nvintendo NES consoles and Sega ...Master Systems - gaming occupies a special place in ...ur lives. But it never felt like we doing or achieving ...omething 'real.' Clearly the entire concept of gaming ...s coming to mean something very different to our youth ...audience. [END]

Note key-chain attached to belt.

Intel outside

28

STYLELAB

For Stylelab's spring/summer 2002 collection we developed a Java applet which converts images into line drawings, evolving over time, and then rewrote it as new code for Shockwave. The result is an image which hints at the underlying source image, but looks more like a torn net-stocking – one of the metaphors we chose for the punk-inspired collection – or a mesh, a metaphor for the web itself.

http://archive.hi-res.net/stylelab

Another aim was to create an audio-ambience which is calm and dulcet, paired with very intense spoken word content and distorted guitars.

The original idea was to use Jello Biafra's lyrics for California über Alles by the Dead Kennedys, but due to the commercial nature of the project he wasn't prepared to grant us permission (bless him) and we chose the poem 'Tale' from Illuminations by Arthur Rimbaud, which transformed the site into a weird and disturbing fairytale.

Contact
Key Retailers
NEW YORK 416 West Broadway NY 10012
LONDON 12 Floral Street Covent Garden Wc2 9DH

2002 F/W Collection
Female
Male

selStyleLab

29

SAW

The promotional site for Saw was our first project for Lionsgate Films after they took over
Artisan Entertainment (who we had done Requiem for a Dream for). Without going too far
into the gory details, the site was designed to reflect the intrigue and the psychological and
voyeuristic nature of the film, without giving the story itself away. As in the film, there is
a time limit within which you should complete the site. It is worth noting that the MPAA
(who rate films for the US market) threatened to withdraw the rating after seeing the
first version of the site we put up. Then we changed all the blood to look
like HP sauce and removed some guns (and some violence) and all was good.

http://archive.hi-res.net/saw

Saw

SHE TOLD ME YOU KNEW ME.

While working on the Punisher site, we had learnt how to make fake blood using food colouring and washing-up liquid. We were using it for a midnight photoshoot in a small alleyway in Shoreditch (London), when out of nowhere a police car appeared. The officers called us over and asked what we were doing (there was fake blood all over the cobbled street) and I started explaining that we were making a website. I will never forget the puzzled look on their faces.

As you can see opposite, it came in *very* handy while working on Saw. We still have a bottle of it under the kitchen sink.

Diesel Heaven

DIESEL HEAVEN

Our second campaign site for Diesel was based around the Autumn/Winter 06 Angels campaign, shot by Terry Richardson. It asked what Diesel people would become once they passed away. Certainly not harp-plucking angels? Out of this, we created Diesel Heaven, heaven's only 7 star hotel, where you can experience the ultimate afterlifestyle and reap the rewards for following Diesel's Guides to Successful Living. You are taken through the site by your host, Delia H. Evans, who picks you up at the lift (no stairs or tunnel for you) to give you the grand tour and show you that true style never ends ...

http://archive.hi-res.net/dieselaw06

SOUVENIRS

dh

NEXT

MENU

THE CONKS
CALLING IN DEAD
DIESEL HEAVEN
EXCLUSIVE

Ugly Betty

Hit U.S. comedy for
Friday Nights
Starts 5 Jan 9.30pm

Fashion has a new face.

"Fashion has a new face"

9.30PM FRIDAY
5TH JANUARY

Ugly Betty
Viral video online ad for Channel 4's launch
of comedy show Ugly Betty

Ugly Betty

Hit U.S. comedy for Friday Nights
Starts 5 Jan 9.30pm

Fashion has a new face.

The Dreamers

32

THE DREAMERS

Often compared to his masterpiece Last Tango in Paris, The Dreamers was introduced as Bernardo Bertolucci's return to form and a celebration of cinema and it's hard to argue. Set in Paris in 1968 amid the student riots, 2 siblings and their American friend hole themselves up in their parent's huge apartment, while they are away, oblivious to the things that take shape around them. The site mirrors this in its structure, allowing you to progress through different rooms in the apartment, which becomes more and more dishevelled the more you discover, until finally the world outside breaks through the window. We got to present it to the man himself, which was an experience in itself.

http://archive.hi-res.net/thedreamers

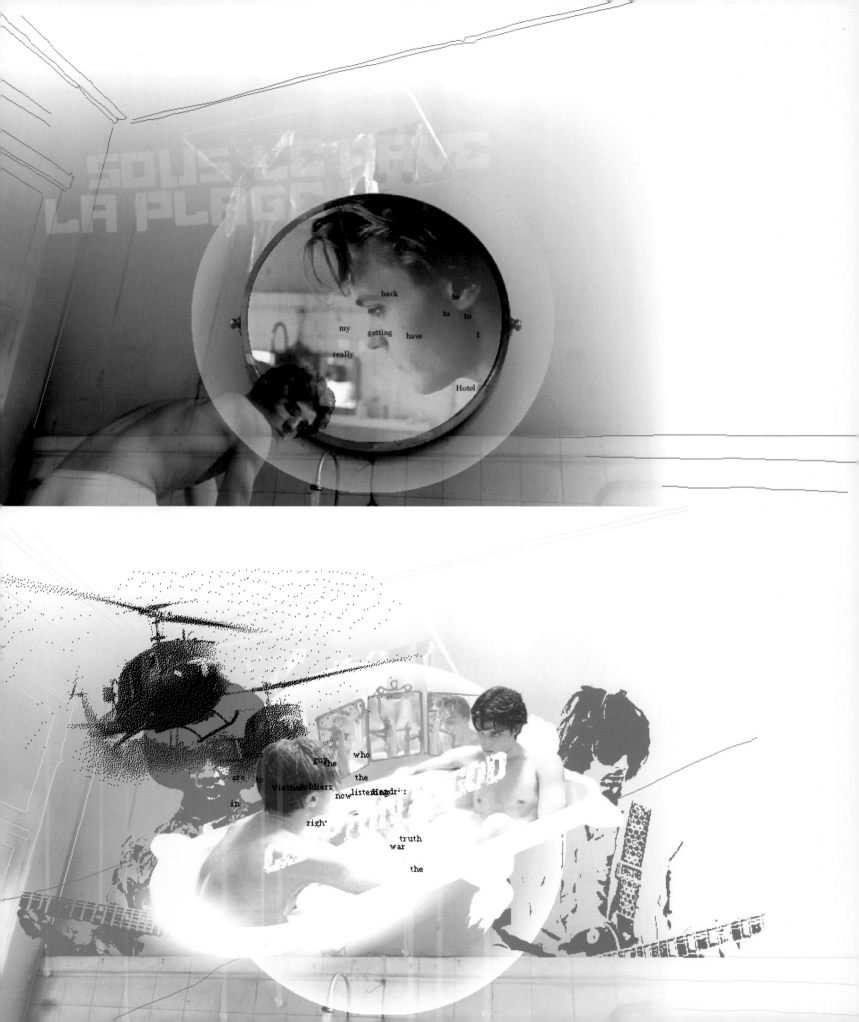

The Dreamers

The Dreamers

33

DIESEL JEWELLERY

To launch Diesel's jewellery collection, we imagined the bizarre world of St Andalou Rousseau-Fontaine, a surrealist jeweller. In his shop he keeps a cabinet in which he locks all his dreams and nightmares, waiting to be explored by an unsuspecting soul, each one focusing on a different jewellery line – his Cabinet of Visions. We collaborated with Geoff Lillemon of Oculart on the dream sequences.

http://archive.hi-res.net/dieseljewellery

BACK

Stores   Overview

BACK

Stores   Overview

Diesel Jewelry
Armorial collection

34

DIESEL JEWELLERY

This Holiday section of the jewellery site keeps us rooted in the universe of Mr Rousseau-Fontaine, the surrealist jeweller. Only this time we focus on another part of his shop, where we come across a book titled The Black Knight and the Calamitous Dragon, which reveals itself to be a very special pop-up book. Once you turn the first page, a whole world explodes out of it, unveiling an animated Christmas tale with a surreal twist.

http://archive.hi-res.net/dieseljewelleryholiday

Return to Collection

Once upon a time, in a land not far from here in a village near a dark forest, there lived a beautiful girl with the greenest emerald eyes.
It was Christmas Eve and she was due to marry the prince of the kingdom the following morning at the castle. It should have been a day of joy, but she was sad, for the marriage had been arranged by her greedy parents. Her true love was an honest local boy – the son of the blacksmith.

Unbeknownst to the prince, the two lovers continued their secret love affair and on this, the eve of the royal wedding, they planned to take their future into their own hands. At the strike of midnight, they were to meet at the forest to leave the village behind and start a new life in a land far away (...)

Excerpt from the The Black Knight and the Calamitous Dragon

Diesel Jewellery
Holiday collection feature

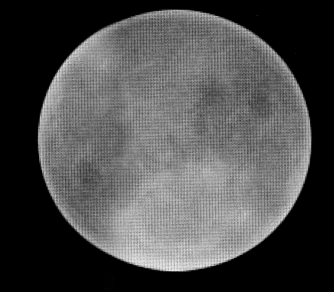

(...) As he stood there, he removed his gauntlet to reveal a black leather-clad hand adorned with a black signet ring, a ring that granted its bearer eternal life. He raised this hand, and the moonlight bounced off its shiny black surface, reflecting the ring's seal into the den as a luminous light. But the lair was empty.

Suddenly from behind he heard a noise. He turned abruptly, and the moonlight flashed off the razor sharp blade as he drew and then plunged the sword into the heart of the dragon which had appeared behind him.

As the dragon slumped to the ground the knight faltered as he looked into the dragons eyes... eyes the colour of greenest emerald. He lifted his visor to reveal his face – the face of the blacksmith's son. The dragon shed a tear and as the tear ran down its face, the dragon burst into a million black stones and where once there was the dragon, lay the beautiful girl.

As she drew her last breath, she looked longingly into the face of her loyal lover, who had spent more then his lifetime searching for her. And so, she closed her eyes for the last time. The knight, head bowed and broken, slipped the ring of eternal life off his finger and was lifted towards the sky.

And his tears turned into snow that covered the village and does so every year on Christmas Eve until the end of time.

Excerpt from the The Black Knight and the Calamitous Dragon

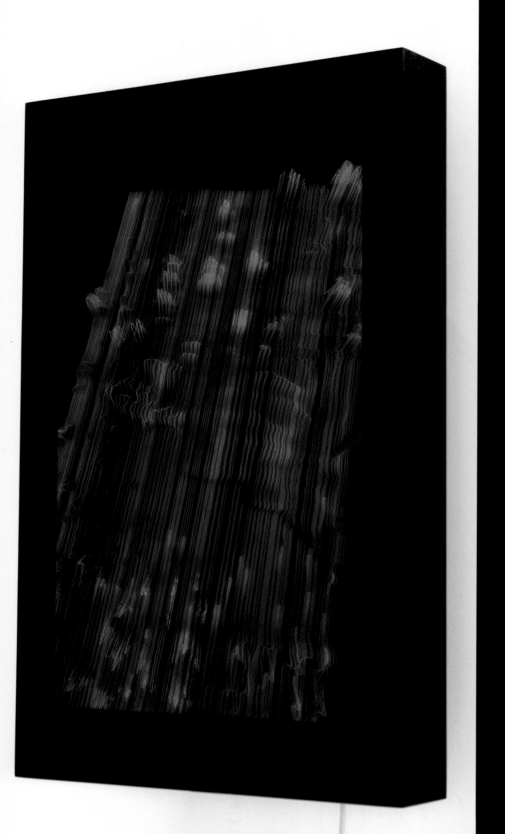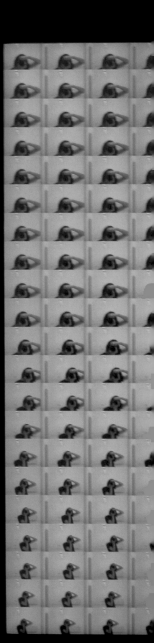

NAN/KA

After years of R&D into alternative ways of interacting with the digital world, we decided to form a new company Nanika *(Japanese for 'something else')* with long-time Hi-ReS! member Andreas Müller to explore interaction between man and machine beyond traditional input and output. And yes, that can involve singing, dancing and flapping your arms as if you had wings – because in our world, you do.

http://www.nanikawa.com

Nanika
Lightboxes

Previous Page
With the Nanika Lightbox project we want to create a
platform of hardware and software that will allow us to
package digital art in a way that takes the complexity out of
owning and displaying it.
We want to take it out of galleries and into spaces you nor-
mally wouldn't see it in, eventually into peoples' homes.
As we've all grown up creating interactive pieces that are
meant to be enjoyed in time frames measured in minutes,
it's liberating to create work and think in terms of years.

Nanika
Wind installation for Nokia flagship stores

Since 2005, we have been working with Nokia on their global Flagship Store project. Our task is to provide interactive content for the stores' freely configurable array of LCD screens.

Mobile phones used to have a simple magic to them when they first came out – for example the fact that you could sit at the beach and talk to someone in a car thousands of miles away. And somehow, it's gone straight to nuissance in recent years.

Our idea was to bring some of the magic back to the mobile phone and allow visitors to the store to use their phones' features to create content for the screens' canvas, in the case of the 'Wind' piece shown above using SMS text messaging to first display your message, then dissolve it into a swirling trail of letters.

Connecting People

Nanika
Wind installation for Nokia flagship stores in situ at New York Store

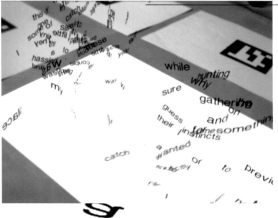

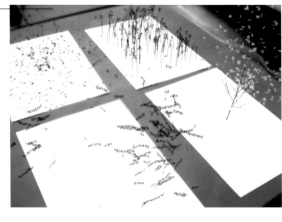

For All Seasons

A piece about memories, seasons – using the elements of the textual representation of the memory to create an interactive one.
This is the result of over a year of late nights and weekends and the desire to completely disregard implementation and current skill level when thinking up the concept for a piece.

As For All Seasons references the A4 paper size, we thought it would be interesting to take it to its logical conclusion. Special markers are printed on pieces of A4 paper and tracked in real time to produce an 'augmented reality' scene showing the 4 memories on screen as if they existed on paper in real space. One day …

Nanika
For All Seasons, augmented reality version

Hi-ReS!
Past, present & future

Founded by
Alexandra Jugovic
Florian Schmitt

Continuously made reality by
Andreas Müller
Andrew Duffus
Amy Harrison
Akane Nakamura
Bela Spahn
Barny Sheeran
Carl Burgess
Erik Jarlsson
George Coltart
Jesse Kanda
Marc Kremers
Nicky Cameron
Sergio Calderon
Tim Ludlow
Theo Tillberg
Tommi Eberwein
Toru Nagahama

Thank you

To all our clients for allowing us to make a living out of something we love and for giving us permission to show the work in this book.

To everyone that has helped us along the way with advice and encouragement.

To Lady Luck for making sure we were at the right place at the right time, doing our thing.

To London. This wouldn't have happened anywhere else.

Hi-Res!
Amantes sunt Amentes

Hi-ReS! the book by hi-res.net

Production management by Janni Milstrey for dgv
Proofreading by English Express
Printed by SIA Livonia Print, Riga

Published by Die Gestalten Verlag, Berlin 2007
ISBN: 978-3-89955-075-7

Bibliographic information published by the Deutsche
Nationalbibliothek. The Deutsche Nationalbibliothek lists
this publication in the Deutsche Nationalbibliografie;
detailed bibliographic data is available on the Internet
at http://dnb.d-nb.de.

For more information please check: www.die-gestalten.de

Respect copyright, encourage creativity!

None of the content in this book was published in exchange
for payment by commercial parties or designers; dgv selected
all included work based solely on its artistic merit.

Amantes sunt Amentes.